SAVING PLANET EARTH

Why agriculture and industry must be
part of the solution

SAVING PLANET EARTH

Why agriculture and industry must be part of the solution

Dr Duncan A. Rouch
Dr David F. Smith
Professor Andrew S. Ball

Connor Court Publishing

PO Box 7257
Redlands Bay Qld 4165
sales@connorcourt.com
www.connorcourt.com

ISBN: 9781925501698 (pbk.)

Cover design by Ian James

Printed in Australia

CONTENTS

ACKNOWLEDGMENTS

Regretfully Dr David F. Smith died during production of this book. Duncan and Andrew are most grateful for David's contribution, and hope this book in part stands as a symbol of his wider contribution to understanding the critical relationship between agriculture and ecology.

For comments on the draft manuscript we are grateful to Mr Doug Gardner (Wannon Water, Australia), Assistant Professor Ben Kefford (University of Canberra, Australia), Jun.-Professor Ralf Schäfer (Universität Koblenz, Landau, Germany) and Dr Min Tang (Hainan University, China). Nevertheless, the authors remain responsible for all views expressed in this book.

FOREWORD

Back in 2006 Duncan and David met for the first time, at the School of Agriculture and Food Systems, University of Melbourne. Duncan had been warned that David was likely to assuredly press his arguments, on a wide range of issues, to any new people around, yet both scientists hit it off immediately. One day, David told a story about his work in Africa to help native farmers improve their productivity. After proving the value of utilising a chemical fertilizer David ran into argument with a 'green' agency manager, who conversely favoured organic fertilizer. Here we recognised two apparently conflicting views on an environmental issue. This became a key symbol to later address, and the story itself became represented in chapter 3.

Early in autumn 2013 Duncan submitted an application for a lectureship job, that included a single paragraph argument about better addressing environmental issues. He didn't get the job, but the paragraph contained embryonic versions of key approaches used in this book.

The following week Duncan called around to visit Andrew at his office, to talk about some ideas to support better response to environmental issues. The first document that came out of our meeting was a single, hand written, page, that concerned deconstructing attitudes of different groups in society toward environmental issues, a result of that first story in 2006. A few days later we met again to discuss the development of arguments, in a short, thirteen-slide, presentation. This provided the first versions of the tables in Chapter 3 that illustrate the different views of people on different relevant parts of society, separated by scale, and identified the missing stakeholders in common discussion, among other additions.

The three authors then spent about 12 months to further develop and research the key ideas and practical proposals, the latter which became chapter 7. Then we began assembling the book, as you see here. It was some journey to find a publisher, so we are grateful to ConnorCourt to agree to publish this book.

Duncan Rouch and Andrew Ball
2 October 2017

1

INTRODUCTION

O n planet earth we are now facing a number of very large
problems relating to the environment of the planet, namely;
the burgeoning human population, the need for increased food
production to feed this population, and the possibility of further
increased climate warming. These three issues combined create
serious implications for the survival of mankind, management of
natural environments and developing sustainable food production systems in the prevailing climate.

For many decades there have been some government responses to environmental matters – mainly pollution and degradation of natural environments. Over the last 50 years, these
responses have generally focused on preserving human health,
such as in clean air and water controls for cities in developed
countries. At the same time, while many environmental activists
have published books to promote environmental conservation,
these books have collectively appeared to have little impact. In
that same 50 years mainstream agriculture and industry have
made significant progress in becoming more sustainable, though
environmental activists have remained heavily critical: to industries they have sharply focussed on only pollution and to agriculture on forest removal. Allied has been criticism of using exotic
plants and animals and eschewing native species in agriculture.

Yet, inherently, mainstream food production has a long and not unpleasant history as a life-giving activity.

The environmental issues resulting from the burgeoning human population have been known for some time, including the effect of increasing human activities in industry and food production, and now the distinct possibility of further increased climate warming. Yet responses have remained slow, with much discussion over the last 50 years and little substantive action. Why have responses been slow? To search for answers to this question we need to examine the attitudes to natural environments of three different sectors in society; environmental supporters, workers in agriculture/industry and those who regulate -in governments. We then need to trace the evolution of these attitudes, and potentially identify causes of the current situation. We also need to remember the common ancestry of ideas about the nature of the environment, which arose from a rather narrow standard definition of what is the environment. With understanding differences in attitudes we should be able to develop a common narrative to be understood by all players and so gain better responses to environmental issues.

So how do we break the impasse in solving natural environmental issues? The key aim is to get environmental activists and industry leaders to respect each other, to hear and understand each other's stories. By breaking down the attitudes of these two groups we can see values on both sides that each can respect. Environmental activists should recognise that agriculture and industry are making significant progress to become more sustainable, while industry leaders should recognise the value of small systems, such as some types of organic farming, as also being sustainable. There is no value for environmental activists to continue to only criticise agriculture and industry, if they wish for these sectors to come to the party for creating a sustainable society. Mutual respect is the way forward.

Also, in a brand new inclusive definition of what are environments, we include human activities including agricultural and industrial activities. Here, these sectors are seen as connected to the environment, so that agricultural and industry leaders can become stakeholders for conserving the global environment.

In this way, we will see more rapid development of sustainable manufacturing and services. Here commercial sustainability directly means staying in business, which in wider terms requires companies to address their environmental footprints. It will also then be easier for governments to better deal with environmental issues.

To begin our story we look at key global challenges, to show the need for better responses to environmental issues (Chapter 2). Then to understand how we got to the current fuzzy and impractical situation we travel back into the 20th century to see where it all started (Chapter 3). By identifying the causes of the impasse in solving natural environmental issues we propose a new approach to environmental management, including a brand new inclusive definition of the environment (Chapter 4). We then look at the place of modern agriculture as a natural descendent of adaptive and conservative management of food plants by early humans (chapter 5). We go on to discuss how manufacturing and service industries can help conserve natural environments while reducing costs (Chapter 6). Finally, we talk about where to from here, including agriculture and industries as key stakeholders to support conservation of natural environmental resources, and the need to build mutual respect between leaders of environmental groups and agriculture and industry leaders (Chapter 7).

2

KEY GLOBAL CHALLENGES

Before investigating the reason for slow responses to environmental issues, we first need to be clear on the reasons for action to better conserve and manage natural environments. So, here we outline the three key global issues; the increasing world population, the global requirement to increase agricultural production and climate change, which together could lead to unsustainable life on planet earth if we do not deal with them effectively.

Increasing world population

The world population has been growing exponentially since the 18th century. In 1804 the world population reached 1 billion and by July 2015 had reached 7.35 billion (23, 24, 25), see Figure 2.1. According to the official United Nations population projections, the world population is projected to increase by almost one billion people within the next twelve years, reaching 8.1 billion in 2025, and to further increase to 9.7 billion in 2050 and 11.2 billion by 2100, according to the medium fertility model. This increase will mostly occur in developing countries. Accelerating rural migration will lead to significant majorities of people living in cities.

Nevertheless, fertility rates vary between countries, and a number countries are expected to see their populations decline by more than 15 per cent by 2050, including Bosnia and Herzegovina, Bulgaria, Croatia, Hungary, Japan, Latvia, Lithuania, Republic of Moldova, Romania, Serbia, and Ukraine. Fertility in all European countries is now below the level required for full replacement of the population in the long run (around 2.1 children per woman, on average), and in the majority of cases, fertility has been below the replacement level for several decades. Fertility for Europe as a whole is projected to increase from 1.6 children per women in 2010-2015 to 1.8 in 2045-2050, but such an increase will not prevent a likely contraction of the total population size.

Population growth, however, remains especially high in the group of 48 countries designated by the United Nations as the least developed countries (LDCs), of which 27 are in Africa. Although the growth rate of the LDCs is projected to slow from its current 2.4 per cent annually, the population of this group is projected to double in size from 954 million inhabitants in 2015 to 1.9 billion in 2050 and further increase to 3.2 billion in 2100. Between 2015 and 2100, the populations of 33 countries, most of them LDCs, have a high probability of at least tripling. Among them, the populations of Angola, Burundi, Democratic Republic of Congo, Malawi, Mali, Niger, Somalia, Uganda, United Republic of Tanzania and Zambia are projected to increase at least five-fold by 2100.

The concentration of population growth in the poorest countries will make it harder for those governments to eradicate poverty and inequality, combat hunger and malnutrition, expand education enrolment and health systems, improve the provision of basic services and implement other elements of a sustainable development agenda to ensure that no-one is left behind.

Importantly, with more people we will likely have more greenhouse gas emissions, certainly require more food production, and further increase the risk of more damage to the natural environments and liveability on planet earth.

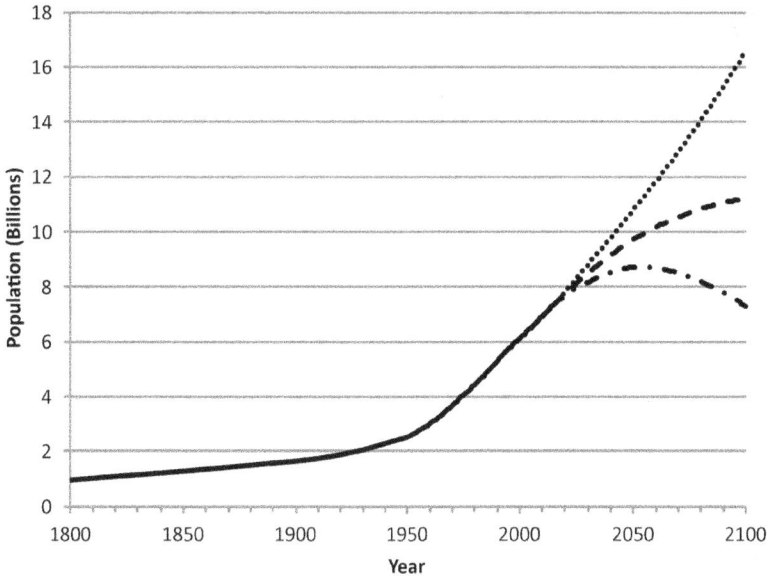

Figure 2.1: World population levels 1800 to 2015 and forward projections 2016 to 2100. Previous population levels, full black line: forecasts; high fertility, dot line; medium fertility, dash line; low fertility, dot-dash line. It is expected on average that in the high fertility model, countries will have the current fertility net levels, between 2.1 and 5 children per woman, dependent on country; for the medium fertility model there will be a decrease to around 2.1 children per woman; and for the low fertility model there will be below 2.1 children per woman. Fertility has continued to fall in the vast majority of countries in the less developed regions, which tends to favour the medium fertility model, which assumes a decline of fertility for developing countries where large families are still prevalent as well as a slight increase of fertility in several countries with fewer than two children per woman on average (23, 24, 25, 26).

Global requirement to increase agricultural production

As a result of continued increases in human population and changes in consumer behaviour agricultural production needs to increase by 60% over the next 40 years to meet rising food demand. People in developing countries are gaining increased incomes, which is resulting in additional incomes being spent to purchase foods, rather than growing food at home. Total arable land is projected to increase only by less than 5% by 2050, so additional production will need to come from increased productivity (21). Since 1945 there has been a linear increase in yields of food crops, such as barley, corn, potato, and rice in developed countries. For example, in the USA potato yields have increased by 4-fold from 94 CWT per acre in 1945 to 412 CWT per acre in 2012, Figure 2.2. This historical rate of increasing yields must continue if we are to meet the required increase in agricultural

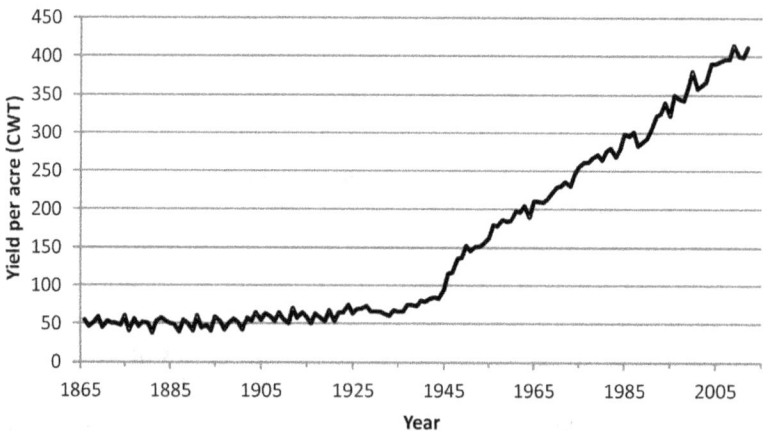

Figure 2.2: **Potato yields in the USA, 1865-2012.** Yield values shown as hundred weight (CWT, 100 pounds) per acre. Since 1945 yields have increased linearly, similarly to many other food crops. The dramatic increases in yields followed as farmers continued to selectively breed new strains and adopt new practices and technologies (18).

products. Also, with higher incomes in developing countries there is a shift to western diets, to include more protein-rich foods, like meat and fish, with further demands on natural environments.

Climate change

Changes in global climates that are reasonably assessed to be caused by human activities are leading to increased global temperatures. The increase in the globally averaged surface temperature from 1850 to 2012, is conservatively +0.78 °C (statistical range 0.72 to 0.85 °C), as reported by the Intergovernmental Panel on Climate Change (IPCC) (13), see Figure 2.3. Between

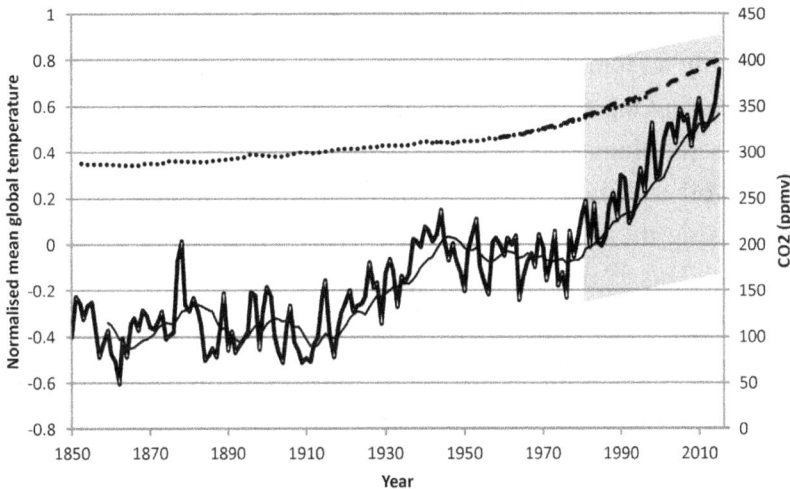

Figure 2.3: Change in global index temperatures and carbon dioxide levels since 1851. This conservatively exhibited co-rises since about 1980, shown by the grey parallelogram. This is consistent with increasing carbon dioxide equivalents causing increasing global temperatures. Index temperatures, thick line and left y axis, are based on the average value in the period 1961-1990, and the trend line, thin line, shows moving decade averages (6, 7): carbon dioxide levels by right y axis, from ice-cores, dotted line (15); direct atmospheric measurements, dashed line (19).

9

1980 and 2010 the average rise in global temperatures has been +0.35 °C per decade.

The increases in global temperatures are due to the increased concentrations of greenhouse gases in the atmosphere, mainly due to emissions from human activities (14). There are two main types of evidence for this conclusion; A) that there has been a consistent co-rise in the levels of greenhouse gases in the atmosphere and global temperatures since about 1980, Figure 2.3; B) it has been independently established that greenhouse gases have properties that would be expected to cause increased global temperatures.

Greenhouse gases include carbon dioxide, methane, nitrous oxide, ozone and some artificial chemicals. Greenhouse gases cause higher temperatures by absorbing energy from the sun and re-radiating the energy to the surface of the earth and lower atmosphere. Human activities – particularly burning fossil fuels (coal, oil and natural gas), agriculture and land clearing – are increasing the concentrations of greenhouse gases in the atmosphere. This is the enhanced greenhouse effect, which is contributing to warming of the Earth. Of the various greenhouse gasses emitted to the atmosphere by human activities, the largest contribution to the rise in surface temperature is caused by the increase in the atmospheric concentration of carbon dioxide gas (13).

Human influence has been detected in five ways; warming of the atmosphere and the ocean, in changes in the global water cycle, in reductions in snow and ice, in global mean sea level rise, and in changes in some climate extremes. Continued emissions of greenhouse gases will cause further warming and changes in all components of the global climate system (land, water and atmosphere). Limiting climate change will require substantial and sustained reductions of greenhouse gas emissions (13).

Changes in climate factors have been observed at local levels. In Australia 13 out of 14 temperature indicators show correlations with increased levels of greenhouse gases (4). For example, the average hottest daily temperature in the decade 2003-2012, 40.7 °C, was 0.9 °C higher than for the long-term average, in 1911-1970. Across the eleven climate zones of China the average temperature for the decade 2003-2012 was 1.0 °C higher than for the average over the period 1951-1970 (2). For India, in the southern areas, below latitude 22° north, show clear increases in both minimum and maximum temperatures since 1980, whereas smaller changes are observed for the northern areas, including mountain regions (11). In this way, it appears that climate change affects the climate of local areas. In the USA climate change is less clear, like northern India. Nevertheless, for the USA changes in three climate indicators correlate with increased levels of greenhouse gases in the atmosphere; namely, minimum temperature, maximum temperature and one-day rainfall (20). For example, since 1980 there has been a trend to larger areas of higher minimum temperatures and smaller areas of lower minimum temperatures, Figure 2.4.

One positive outcome of climate change has been an increase in growing seasons. In Australia the average period of the growing season in the decade 2001-2010 was 226 days, 23 days higher than the long term average over 1911-1970 (5). A similar increase has been observed in the UK (9).

Increased global temperatures also lead to increased sea levels. The mean rate of global averaged sea level rise was 1.7 millimetres per year between 1901 and 2010 (statistical range 1.5

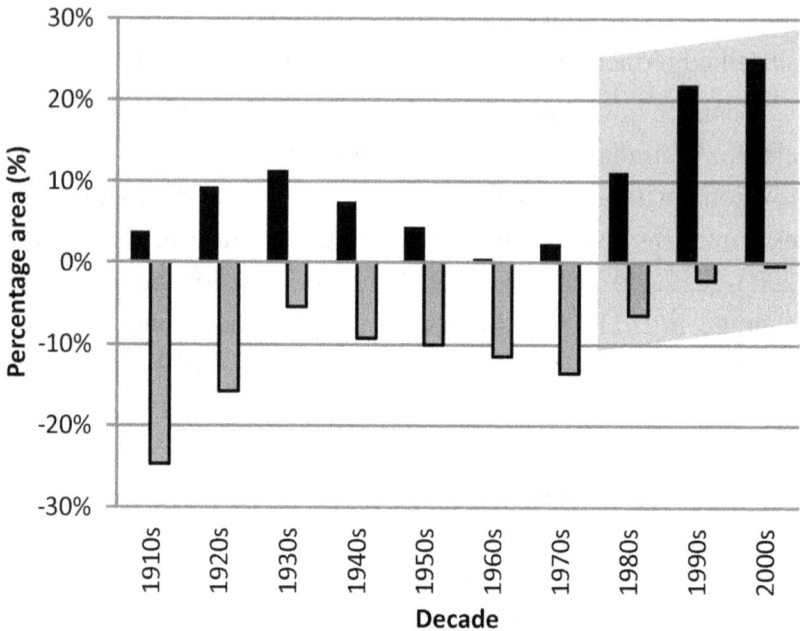

Figure 2.4: Increases in minimum temperatures in the USA. Data for the mainland, not including Alaska and Hawaii. Average areas of USA with much below-normal (grey bars, negative numbers) and much above-normal (black bars, positive numbers) monthly mean minimum temperatures for decades, 1911 to 2010. Since 1980 a trend to both larger areas of higher minimum temperatures and smaller areas of lower minimum temperatures has occurred, marked by grey parallelogram (20).

to 1.9 millimetres per year). Since the early 1970s, about 75% of the observed rise in global mean sea level is explained by the combination of glacier mass loss and ocean thermal expansion from warming (13).

In recent times fatalities and economic losses associated with natural disasters have been higher in developed countries. During the period from 1970 to 2008, over 95% of deaths from extreme weather, climate, and geophysical events occurred in developing countries. Middle-income countries with rapidly expanding asset bases have borne the largest economic burden of natural disasters. During the period from 2001 to 2006, losses amounted to about 1% of GDP for middle-income countries, while this ratio has been about 0.3% of GDP for low-income countries and less than 0.1% of GDP for high-income countries. In small exposed countries, particularly small island developing states, losses expressed as a percentage of GDP have been particularly high, exceeding 1% in many cases, and 8% in the most extreme cases. The frequency of these disasters is likely to increase in the future as further greenhouse gas production is likely to more frequently promote extreme weather events (12).

Given the likely serious effects of increased climate change the IPCC has also forecasted future changes in climate using a large range of computer models (3, 13). These models simulate alterations in climate based on a set of scenarios with different changes in emissions of greenhouse gasses from human activities. The IPCC has forecasted changes in both the short term and longer term. In the short term the average global surface temperature change for the period 2016–2035, relative to 1986–2005, will likely be in the range of plus 0.3 °C to 0.7 °C. Further increases of the human population is likely to be a factor in increasing emissions of greenhouse gasses in the future

The longer term assessed covered the period 2081–2100 relative to 1986–2005. In modelling changes in the longer term four scenarios were used, with atmospheric levels of carbon dioxide equivalents of greenhouse gases forecast to peak at; scenario 1) 490 ppm before 2100 and then decline, 2) 650 ppm by 2100 and remain at this level, 3) 850 ppm by 2100 and remain at this level, and 4) at least 1370 ppm by 2100 and continue rising, see Figure 2.5. The global atmosphere currently has about 400 ppm of carbon dioxide equivalents of greenhouse gases. Scenario 4 has the current trajectory, 'business as usual', that is if there is no significant reduction of producing greenhouse gases in the near future. Scenario 1 would require halting most greenhouse emissions, which, if relying on current government policies, is unlikely to occur. The forecast increases in average global surface temperatures for the four scenarios by year 2100 are 1) 1.0 °C (range 0.3 °C to 1.7 °C); 2) 1.9 °C (range 1.1°C to 2.6 °C); 3) 2.3 °C (range 1.4 °C to 3.1 °C); and 4) 3.7 °C (range 2.6 °C to 4.8 °C) (13).

Another way to look at the effect of increasing levels of greenhouse gases on climate is to assess when average annual temperatures exceed the bounds of historical variability, that is, when temperatures increase and remain beyond normal historical ranges in every subsequent year. For scenario 2 average annual temperatures would exceed the bounds of historical variability by year 2069 (statistical range 2051 to 2087) and for scenario 4, 'business as usual', by year 2047 (statistical range 2033 to 2061) (16). These are both well before the year 2100, discussed above as a point to show differences between different scenarios, and point to the importance of significantly decreasing emissions of greenhouse gases as soon as possible.

At the current rate of increasing global temperatures it is likely that +2 °C could be reached in only 40 years from now. It is virtually certain that there will be more frequent hot and fewer cold temperature extremes over most land areas on daily and seasonal timescales as global mean temperatures increase. It is also very likely that atmospheric heat waves will occur with a higher frequency and duration. Least developed countries will wear the

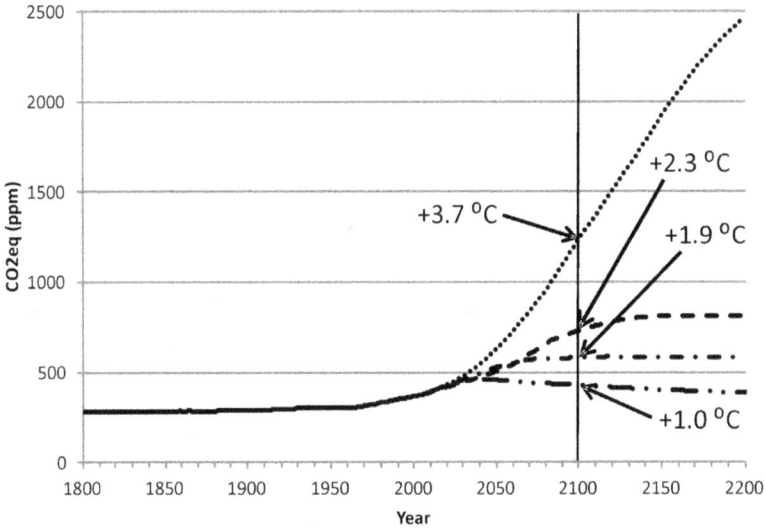

Figure 2.5: Global carbon dioxide equivalent levels of greenhouse gases 1800 to 2005 and four forecast models. Previous levels 1800 to 2005, black line: four forecast levels, 2006 to 2200, for models; 1 (dot-dot-dash line), 2 (dot-dash line), 3 (dash line), 4 (dot line). Forecast average increased global temperature values at year 2100 are shown for each model. See text for descriptions of forecast models (16).

brunt of the increased frequency of extreme weather disasters, in both terms of loss of human life and financial costs (28).

The Arctic region will warm more rapidly than the global average, and average warming over land will be larger than over the ocean. Clearly continued emissions of greenhouse gases will cause further warming and changes in all components of the climate system. Limiting climate change will require substantial and sustained reductions of greenhouse gas emissions.

Global mean sea level rise for 2081–2100, relative to 1986–2005, will likely be in the ranges for scenario 1) 0.26 to 0.55 m; 2) 0.32 to 0.63 m 3) 0.33 to 0.63 m; and 4) 0.45 to 0.82 m (medium confidence ranges). For scenario 4 the forecast rise by the year

2100 is 0.52 to 0.98 m (medium confidence range). It is virtually certain that global mean sea level rise will continue beyond 2100, with sea level rises due to thermal expansion to continue for many centuries (13).

In line with IPCC modelling many states and local governments in Australia have conservatively benchmarked sea level rises, as 0.3 - 0.4 m by 2050, and 0.8 - 0.9 m by 2100 (1). Higher sea levels are likely to lead to losses of coastal shoreline land. For example, at Wooli Wooli Beach, New South Wales, Australia, the forecast loss of coastal land is -10 to -80 m by 2100, depending on specific location (20). Also, there will be corresponding increased flood hazards from coastal rivers, which has resulted in deepening restrictions on building near coast and coastal rivers, such as in the state of New South Wales, Australia (6). In this case, new buildings should be located above the flood line forecast for 2100.

Increased levels of carbon dioxide in the atmosphere also contribute to acidification of oceans due to absorption of carbon dioxide. It is estimated that oceans have absorbed about half the excess carbon dioxide released by human activities in the past 200 years. As carbon dioxide is absorbed from the atmosphere it interacts with sea water to form carbonic acid. To date this absorbed carbon dioxide is resulting in chemical changes in the ocean, and is estimated to have caused a decrease in oceanic pH of 0.1. This is referred to as ocean acidification as the oceans are becoming more acidic (though technically they are still alkaline).

In the long-term ocean acidification is likely to be the most significant impact of a changing climate on marine ecosystems, such as the Great Barrier Reef, located by the north-eastern coast of Australia (10). The main reason for this conclusion is that carbonic acid, produced by absorbed carbon dioxide, decreases the capacity of reef's corals to build skeletons and other sea animals to build shells.

This occurs as carbonic acid releases a bicarbonate ion and a hydrogen ion. The hydrogen ion bonds with free carbonate ions in the water forming another bicarbonate ion. As a result, there is fall in levels of free carbonate ions. This means there is less carbonate available to marine animals for making calcium carbonate shells and skeletons. Even relatively small increases in ocean acidity decrease the capacity of corals to build skeletons, which in turn decreases their capacity to create habitats for the reef's marine life. From a current pH of 8.2, it is predicted that the ocean's pH could fall to about 7.8 by 2100, with likely devastating consequences for reef-based marine life.

Given the likely serious impacts of climate change it will be essential to manage the risks of climate change, which involves adaptation and mitigation decisions with substantial implications for future generations, economies, and environments (14). In assessing the financial costs of climate change indications are that the costs of adapting economic and infrastructure systems are less than the costs of inaction. For example, if we do not adapt we will still have to more frequently pay for immediate responses to the effects of extreme weather events. In contrast, cooperation between different countries for reducing emissions of greenhouse gases at regional levels, such as east Asia, could lower the costs of reducing emissions by as much as 25%. Regional cooperation would also spread the cost of developing both low carbon technologies and design standards for proofing buildings and infrastructures against future climate change (27).

Reducing the vulnerability of developing countries to climate change can be addressed by attention to reducing poverty and improvement of education, nutrition, health and safe housing along with robust settlement structures (28). For all countries reducing exposure to climate hazards will require disaster risk management, which will include early warning systems, improved building codes and practices, coastal land exclusion zones for buildings, robust transport and road infrastructure, robust wastewater treatment systems and diversified water resources.

Conserving natural resources will be important for improving food production, maintaining quality of life and natural ecosystems while reducing the stress of climate change on these. Adapting food production to climate change will also include options like advanced crop and animal varieties and efficient irrigation of crops as well as conservation of resources. Effective management of natural resources, required to continue support of life on planet earth, will involve restoration of damaged soils, fresh water and marine ecosystems, along with reforestation and creating new forests. Changes in governments and societies attitudes will lead these approaches for adapting to climate change.

Together the changes in climate, population and food production have fundamentally serious implications for conserving the natural environment.

Conclusion

Here on planet earth we are now facing three serious issues, namely; the burgeoning human population, the need for increased food production to feed the growing human population, and climate warming, which may well lead to more serious implications for stable climate and management of natural environments.

Yet, it has it been difficult to get good responses to natural environmental issues over many decades. So, how do we gain better responses to help preserve the quality of life on planet earth for future generations? To answer this question we must looked at both sides of the impasse, with supporters of the natural environment on one side and industry and government on the other.

References

1. Antarctic Climate & Ecosystems Cooperative Research Centre (2011) Government coastal planning responses to rising sea levels, Australia and overseas. http://www.acecrc.org.au, accessed 28-10-14.

2. Beijing Climate Center. China Meteorological Administration, State Council of the People's Republic of China (2013) Monitoring data. http://bcc.cma.gov.cn, accessed 30-12-13.

3. Bernie. D. (2010) Temperature implications from the IPCC 5th assessment Representative Concentration Pathways (RCP). Work stream 2, Report 11 of the AVOID programme (AV/WS2/D1/R11). http://www.metoffice.gov.uk, accessed 20-12-13.

4. Bureau of Meteorology, Australian Government (2013a) Australian climate extremes – Time series graphs. Index various. http://www.bom.gov.au, accessed 8-1-14.

5. Bureau of Meteorology, Australian Government (2013b) Australian climate extremes – Time series graphs. Index growing season length. http://www.bom.gov.au, accessed 8-1-14.

6. Cowtan, K., Way, R. G. (2014a) Coverage bias in the HadCRUT4 temperature series and its impact on recent temperature trends. *Quarterly Journal of the Royal Meteorological Society,* 140: 1935-1944, July 2014 B, DOI:10.1002/qj.2297.

7. Cowtan, K., Way, R. G. (2014b) Coverage bias in the HadCRUT4 temperature series and its impact on recent temperature trends.

UPDATE Temperature reconstruction by domain: version 2.0 temperature series. http://www-users.york.ac.uk, accessed 6-8-15.

8. Department of Planning, New South Wales, Australia (2010) NSW Coastal Planning Guideline: Adapting to Sea Level Rise. http://www.planning.nsw.gov.au, accessed 11-10-13.

9. Department of Energy & Climate Change, UK (2013) Thermal growing season in central England. https://www.gov.uk, accessed 28-12-13.

10. Hoegh-Guldberg, O. Anthony, K., Berkelmans, R., Dove, S., Fabricus, K., Lough, J., Marshall, P. van Oppen, M. J. H., Negri, A. and Willis, B. (2007). Vulnerability of reef-building corals on the Great Barrier Reef to climate change, Chapter 10. In *Climate Change and the Great Barrier Reef,* eds. Johnson, J. E. and Marshall, P.A. Great Barrier Reef Marine Park Authority and Australian Greenhouse Office, Australia. http://www.gbrmpa.gov.au, accessed 28-10-14.

11. Indian Institute Of Tropical Meteorology, Ministry of Earth Sciences, Government of India (2013) Meteorological Data Sets. http://www.tropmet.res.in, accessed 29-12-13.

12. IPCC (2012) Summary for Policymakers. In *Managing the Risks of Extreme Events and Disasters to Advance Climate Change Adaptation,* eds. Field, C.B., V. Barros, T.F. Stocker, D. Qin, D.J. Dokken, K.L. Ebi, M.D. Mastrandrea, K.J. Mach, G.-K. Plattner, S.K. Allen, M. Tignor, and P.M. Midgley. Working Groups I and II of the Intergovernmental Panel on Climate Change. Cambridge University Press, Cambridge, UK, and New York, NY, USA, pp. 3-21. https://www.ipcc-wg1.unibe.ch, accessed 16-12-13.

13. IPCC (2013) Summary for Policymakers. In *Climate Change 2013: The Physical Science Basis.* Contribution of Working Group I to the Fifth Assessment Report of the Intergovernmental Panel on Climate Change, eds. Stocker, T.F., D. Qin, G.-K. Plattner, M. Tignor, S. K. Allen, J. Boschung, A. Nauels, Y. Xia, V. Bex and P.M. Midgley. Cambridge University Press, Cambridge, United

Kingdom and New York, NY, USA. http://www.climate2013.org, accessed 12-12-13.

14. IPCC (2014) Summary for Policymakers. In *Climate Change 2014: Impacts, Adaptation, and Vulnerability*, eds. Paulina Aldunce, P., J. P. Ometto, N. Raholijao and K. Yasuhara. http://www.ipcc-wg2.gov, accessed 28-10-14.

15. MacFarling Meure, C., Etheridge,D., Trudinger, C., Steele, P., Langenfelds, R., van Ommen, T., Smith, A., and Elkins, J. (2006) Law Dome CO_2, CH_4 and N_2O ice core records extended to 2000 years BP. *Geophysical Research Letters*, 33: L14810, doi:10.1029/2006GL026152.

16. Meinshausen, M., Smith, S. J., Calvin, K., Daniel, J. S., Kainuma, M. L. T., Lamarque, J-F., Matsumoto, K., Montzka, S. A., Raper, S. C. B., Riahi, K., Thomson, A., Velders, G. J. M., van Vuuren, D. P. P. (2011) The RCP greenhouse gas concentrations and their extensions from 1765 to 2300. *Climatic Change*, 109(1-2): 213-241. DOI: 10.1007/s10584-011-0156-z. Data taken from http://tntcat.iiasa.ac.at:8787, accessed 28-10-14.

17. Mora, C., Frazier, A.G., Longman, R.J., Dacks, R.S. Maya M. Walton, M.M., Tong, E.J., Sanchez, J.J., Kaiser, L.R., Stender, Y.O., Anderson, J.M., Ambrosino, C.M., Fernandez-Silva, I. Giuseffi, L.M. and Giambelluca, T.W. (2013) The projected timing of climate departure from recent variability. *Nature*, 502: 183-187.

18. National Agricultural Statistics Service, United States Department of Agriculture (12-4-2013) Historical Track Record – Crop Production. http://usda.mannlib.cornell.edu, accessed 14-2-14.

19. National Oceanic and Atmospheric Administration, USA (2016). NOAA ESRL DATA ftp://aftp.cmdl.noaa.gov, accessed 12-12-16.

20. National Oceanic and Atmospheric Administration, National Climatic Data Center, USA (2013) U.S. Climate Extremes Index (CEI). http://www.ncdc.noaa.gov, accessed 8-1-14.

21. OECD (2012) OECD-FAO Agricultural Outlook 2012-2021. http://www.keepeek.com, accessed 28-10-14.

22. Rollason, V., Patterson, D., and Huxley, C. (2010) Assessing Shoreline Response to Sea Level Rise: An Alternative to The Bruun Rule. http://www.coastalconference.com, accessed 11-10-13.

23. United Nations, Department of Economic and Social Affairs, Population Division (1999) *The World at Six Billion.* ESA/P/WP.154. Data from http://www.un.org/esa/population, accessed 28-10-14.

24. United Nations, Department of Economic and Social Affairs, Population Division (2015a) *World Population Prospects: The 2015 Revision, Key Findings and Advance Tables.* Working Paper No. ESA/P/WP.241.

25. United Nations, Department of Economic and Social Affairs, Population Division (2015b) *World Population Prospects: The 2015 Revision, Methodology of the United Nations Population Estimates and Projections,* Working Paper No. ESA/P/WP.242.

26. United Nations, Department of Economic and Social Affairs, Population Division (2015c) *World Population Prospects: The 2015 Revision,* [Data file: total population –both sexes]. https://esa.un.org/unpd/wpp/Download/Standard/Population/, accessed 4-1-17.

27. Westphal, M.I, Hughes, G.A., Brömmelhörster, J. (2013) Economics of Climate Change in East Asia. Mandaluyong City, Philippines: Asian Development Bank. http://www.adb.org, accessed 28-10-14.

28. World Bank Group (2006) *Managing Climate Risk. Integrating Adaptation into World Bank Group Operations.* Global Environment Facility Program. http://siteresources.worldbank.org, accessed 29-12-13.

3

LESSONS FROM THE PAST

Why has it been hard to get responses to natural environmental issues?

It is now urgent to gain an effective answer to the question, why has it been hard to get responses to natural environmental issues? If answered, we might gain better responses to help preserve the quality of life on planet earth for future generations. To answer this question we look at both sides of the impasse, with environmentalist supporters of the natural environment on one side and industry and government on the other. Many environmentalists tend to think that the problem is simply that industry and government do not properly recognise the values of the natural environment. On the other side, many industry and government leaders recognise the importance of conserving the natural environment yet many find it difficult to give enough priority to this against the array of other important issues. To get better responses we argue there must be changes to attitudes on both sides. How did we get to this view?

Some years ago an agricultural expert volunteered to travel to Africa to help local farmers improve their yields in growing crops, as part of a project financed by an international aid agency. He had advised local farmers to use chemical fertilisers in a controlled way, including simple tests to determine the minimum amount of fertilizer to use, to improve yields of their crops. Later the farmers were visited by an officer of the agency who advised the farmers not to use the chemical fertilizer, as the farmer should use an organic fertilizer for sustainable use. Like any case there are two sides. On one hand, chemical fertilisers are ordinarily not-renewable which favours use of renewable organic fertilisers. On the other hand, organic fertilisers produce a substantially lower yield compared to chemical fertilisers and are generally scarce in rural areas of Africa. Also, key plant nutrients, namely phosphate, nitrogen and potassium, have limited and variable concentrations in organic fertilisers. So, is it really acceptable to deny poor African farmers the same optimum resources as available to farmers in developed countries? Had the view of the aid agency officer been too narrowly focussed on conservation of natural environments to be of practical use?

Another common view amongst natural environmental activists is that the perfect place to live is a small village. While we shall not deny a personal choice for someone to live in a village, can we really expect 8, 9 or 10 billion people on planet earth to all live in villages?

From the two views noted above we are beginning to see that the position of natural environmental activists may not provide all the answers. Also, out on the worldwide web it can be difficult to see exactly what these people stand for. We have seen the growing fog of partial arguments and lack of practical conclusions over the last 40 years. Where are the clear statements of principles? How do we get there? Yet one thing is clear, many of these people blame modern conventional agriculture and industries for degradation of environmental areas and the loss of biodiversity.

We do not deny the pollution and degradation of natural environments by parts of main-stream agriculture and industries over many years. On the other hand, if we really wanted to preserve natural environments, wouldn't it be better to have all stakeholders on board, including mainstream agriculture and industries? A good example of this is improved farm management under the Potter Farmland Plan, in Australia, which encourages farmers to plant trees and move fence lines to overcome erosion and salinity and improve land quality (4). Are you also wondering why we have put 'natural' in front of 'environment' and 'environmental activists' when this is generally assumed? This is a clue to understanding the poor responses to natural environmental issues, which we will unroll later in this book.

Lessons from the past

To better understand the impasse, with supporters of the natural environment on one side and industry and government on the other, we need to look at the historic development of key ideas about conserving the environment.

Back in the 19ᵗʰ century people began writing about the conservation of wild nature and the increase of what is well described as the industrial society. In 1854 Henry Thoreau published a hymn for living in wild nature, titled *Walden; or, Life in the Woods* (29). Here nature only changed by season. Forester and ecologist Aldo Leopold argued, in 1949, that a responsible relationship must exist between people and the land they inhabit (17). He wrote to promote wider appreciation of wild nature and to stress that humans must have respect for the Earth.

In the 1960's natural environmental scientists first signalled the increasing destruction of the natural environment by human domestic and industrial chemicals and waste. For example, Rachel Carson documented detrimental effects of pesticides on the environment, particularly on birds, in her book *Silent Spring*, published in 1962 (2).

In 1972 five prominent ecologists, Edward Goldsmith, Robert Allen, Michael Allaby, John Davoll, and Sam Lawrence, published a radical response to the human degradation of the natural environment, *A Blueprint for Survival* (10). This contained a sweeping proposal for immediate action to halt environmental destruction, which was supported by 34 distinguished biologists, ecologists, doctors and economists of the day. While their proposal received a lot of fanfare, there was not much following action by governments. Why not? Some of reasons to answer this question lie in the details of the proposal.

Firstly, we consider the definition of environment quoted by the five ecologists, "The environment is a system which includes all living things and the air, water and soil which is their habitat." This is a simple initial definition, derived from the works by earlier supporters for the primacy of wild nature. This definition, however, implicitly only includes nature and therefore excludes humans and our manmade adaptations of the natural environment, such as the managed ecosystems called agriculture. For industry and governments the natural environment is then often seen as 'out there', separate, that is, somewhat disconnected from mainstream society.

Secondly, the natural environment was seen as stable, based on self-regulating processes, "… all ecosystems tend towards stability, and further that the more diverse and complex the ecosystem the more stable it is; that is, the more species there are, and the more they interrelate, the more stable is their environment. By stability is meant the ability to return to the original position after any change, instead of being forced into a totally different pattern – and hence predictability." Similarly, in the 1970s James Lovelock developed the Gaia hypothesis, stating that organisms interact with their inorganic surroundings on Earth to form a self-regulating, complex system that contributes to maintaining the conditions for life on the planet (18, 19).

Following these views school teachers educated during late 1960's and early 1970s were likely to see 'The Environment' as the natural system 'out there' consisting of mountains, rivers, plains, forests, wild flowers, beautiful native animals and industrious insects, and that all these elements cosily interacted with each other in classic homeostatic ecology. For previous generations most students were likely to learn this view. Some of these students became environmental activists of following generations and some of these students became teachers for future generations.

Also, following books published over many years by ecologists and other supporters of the natural environment, such as *The Great U-Turn*, by Edward Goldsmith (11), and *Here on Earth -An argument for hope*, by Tim Flannery (8), have generally continued with little change from the 1972 position. Historians of environmental issues, such as Alfred Crosby in his book, *Ecological Imperialism: The Biological Expansion of Europe, 900-1900*, have also questioned the relations between human agency and the transformation of the globe's natural environments through imperialism, exploration, increased agricultural efficiency, technological innovation and urban expansion (5).

In these books industries' contribution to society is often only discussed in terms of pollution. The contribution of agriculture is often first introduced as the major cause of forest removal. However, these authors may recognise that natural changes can occur in ecosystems, so are not as stable as first proposed.

Over history shifts in ecosystems across space and time must have occurred due to the shift in environmental conditions, such as planet cooling with glaciation, and development of new species over time. Changes in ecosystems are, therefore, not necessarily destructive, but adaptive. Also, a number of environmental activists believe that degraded environments should be restored with natural assemblages of plants and animals that existed at some point in the past, based on historical information. However, this approach has been repeatedly challenged by ecologists (27). For example, Roy Hobbs and colleagues state that land conversion, climate change and species invasions are contributing to the widespread emergence of novel ecosystems, which demand a shift in how we think about traditional approaches to conservation, restoration and environmental management (12). Natural gain is an application of this thinking to agriculture in southern Australia (25). Nevertheless, we need to know if a change in an environmental factor is dangerous or not, whether for a natural, built, agricultural or industrial environment.

Influence of the past on current views

The initial narrow definitions of environment and ecosystems have clearly been the basis for discussion, arguments and demands from environmental activists over many decades. As a result of these views mainstream agriculture and industry have generally been put off-side by environmental activists. Also, as a result of these narrow views, industrial companies have often tended not see themselves as being part of the natural environment, so why worry? Additionally, governments have tended to see the natural environment as being peripheral to main priorities.

A corollary of the initial narrow definitions is that industry reports on improving their responses to environmental issues have gone under the radar. For example, in Australia two reports, *Environmental Sustainability and Industry: Road to a sustainable future*, and, *Environmental Sustainability: An Industry Response*, were published in the previous decade (13, 28). These reports, however, apparently did not receive any public support from environmental associations or activists.

In terms of getting better responses to environmental challenges, how much is the public support for better responses and how has this changed over the last two decades? We can get an answer by looking at the serial surveys of public attitudes to the natural environment by the International Social Survey Programme (ISSP), in over 30 countries around the world (14, 15, 16, 30). These surveys have been run three times so far, in 1993, 2000 and 2010, with the last time occurring during the global financial crisis (GFC), which may have negatively affected public views. While there are common environmental issues across different countries, there are also country specific factors, such as different economic stability and standards of living. So, it is important to look at data from different countries in detail. Here we discuss data from four countries, England, The United States of America, Canada, and Australia. The economies of last two countries effectively survived the GFC without serious issues, unlike England and the United States.

People were asked about their personal approach to address environmental issues in their lives. For example, to respond to the statement, "It is just too difficult for someone like me to do much about the environment". In this case the majority of people in all four countries disagreed, over all three interview years. In responding to the opposite statement, "I do what is right for the environment, even when it costs more money or takes more time", the majority of people in all four countries agreed, as expected from their response to the first question, again over all three interview years.

People were also asked about how they would personally pay to protect the environment, either through higher prices, higher taxes or cuts in standard of living. Generally, people were happy to pay higher prices, except for England in 2010, see Figure 3.1. In all four countries in 1993 there was almost equal agreement to pay higher taxes compared to disagreement, but by 2000 the majority disagreed, which continued in 2010. In general, the majority of people were not willing to have cuts in their standard of living, especially in England and the United States. In 1993, for both Australia and Canada, a majority of people said they were willing to have cuts in their standard of living, but by 2000 this had fallen away. Nevertheless, we see that many people gave their personal support to address environmental issues, to the point that they agreed they would pay higher prices to protect the natural environment.

When people were asked to compare the importance of environmental issues to economic issues there were changes in support. The survey asked people to respond to the statement. "We worry too much about the future of the environment and not enough about prices and jobs today". In both England and the USA in 1993 and 2000 more people disagreed with this statement than agreed, however by 2010 more people agreed than

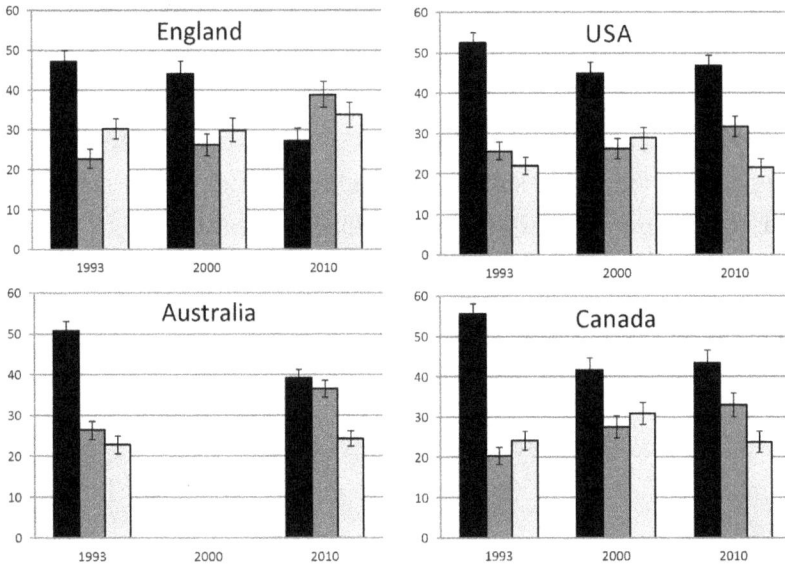

Figure 3.1 Responses to the question, 'How willing would you be to pay much higher prices in order to protect the environment?'. Willing (%), dark black bars; Unwilling (%), grey bars; Neither willing nor unwilling (%), pale grey bars. Responses shown for survey years 1993, 2000 and 2010. Error bars mark 95% confidence limits. Australia did not report data for 2000. Data from IPSS (14, 15, 16, 30).

disagreed, especially in England, see Figure 3.2. This decrease in support for addressing environmental issues, compared to economic issues, followed the GFC. For countries seriously affected by the GFC, like England and the USA, it appears reasonable to suggest that, once the economies of these countries pick up after the GFC, that public support for dealing with environmental issues will substantially improve.

In Canada, which did not experience major economic issues during the GFC, the majority of people disagreed with the survey statement in all three survey years, and therefore the public in Canada continue to give primary support to address environmental problems. In Australia, however, while the majority of people disagreed with the survey statement in 1993, by 2010 this had fallen down.

We can more closely examine the fall in support for addressing environmental issues in Australia, by looking at the serial surveys of public attitudes to the natural environment,

Who Cares about the Environment?, in New South Wales, Australia (20), which covers the same time period as the international surveys.

In the serial surveys from 1994 to 2012 people were also asked to rate their level of concern about environmental problems, see Figure 3.3. While public support remained high dur-

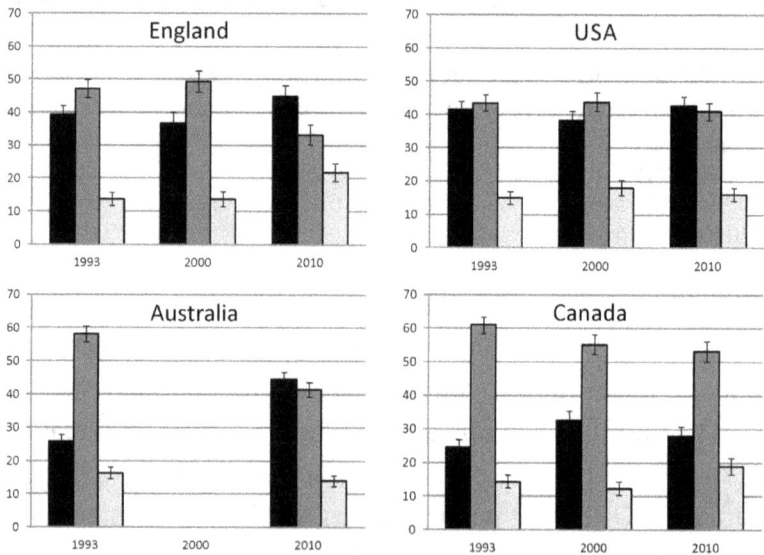

Figure 3.2 Responses to the statement, 'We worry too much about the future of the environment and not enough about prices and jobs today'. Willing (%), dark black bars; Unwilling (%), grey bars; Neither willing nor unwilling (%), pale grey bars. For survey years 1993, 2000 and 2010. Error bars mark 95% confidence limits. Australia did not report data for 2000. Data from IPSS (14, 15, 16, 30).

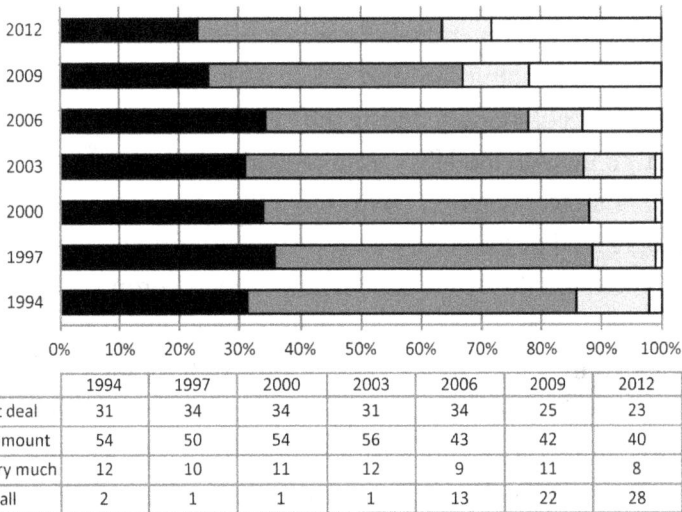

	1994	1997	2000	2003	2006	2009	2012
■ A great deal	31	34	34	31	34	25	23
▨ A fair amount	54	50	54	56	43	42	40
☐ Not very much	12	10	11	12	9	11	8
☐ Not at all	2	1	1	1	13	22	28

Figure 3.3. Decline in public support for conservation of natural environments in Australia. Note, prior to 2006, survey participants were asked to rate their level of concern about environmental problems on a four-point scale ranging from 'a great deal' to 'not at all'. Since 2006 the question has been split into two parts (20).

ing 1994 to 2003, there was continuing decline through 2006 to 2012. The percentage of people with either no or not very much concern for environmental problems were relatively stable, 11 to 14%, across 1994 to 2003, but then increased to 23% in 2006, 33% in 2009, and 36% in 2012. So, by 2012 more than a third of respondents gave virtually no support to fixing environmental problems.

Given that the Australian economy survived the GFC without major problems there is likely a different reason for the fall in public support there for better responding to environmental issues. It is then reasonable to suggest that the fall in public support is due to political reasons.

A contributing factor to the malaise in public support for conserving environments is the culture of contentment (9). The current sense of contentment in a range of western countries stems from the economic comfort achieved by the fortunate, politically dominant community during the 1980s. Countries affected by this culture include the USA, England and Australia, while Denmark is a notable exception. With the culture of contentment affluent people tend to see personal virtue in their fortune rising over time, even though this follows general economic growth. These people tend to focus on narrow short-term needs, to which politicians respond in similar terms. As a result, we have the politics of contentment, in which different political parties vie for votes from the affluent middle and upper-middle classes using short-term policy proposals. Who they ignore are the working underclass, which are denied political voice, and what they ignore are long-term issues. In terms of philosophy, major political parties, from both the left and right, have jettisoned principles in the moved toward the centre right, in their focus on short term needs of the affluent class. This includes an over focus on government deficits, at the expense of better investing in the future, as argued by John Edwards, board member of the Australian Reserve Bank (1).

As a result, over the last 10 years in Australia, in particular, we have seen a lack of discussion and agreement about how to respond to climate change by the two major political parties. After much promising, but hardly any public discussion an emissions trading scheme was set up by the Labor government in 2011, but was cancelled in 2014 by the Liberal government (24). Emissions trading, or cap and trade, is a market-based approach used to control pollution, in this case greenhouse gases, by providing economic incentives for achieving reductions in the emissions of pollutants. Without clear leadership for responding to environmental issues, an increasing number of self-interested people have decided that conservation of the natural environment is not important to their own lives.

By contrast, in Canada the Conservative Party, which had been in government from 2006 to 2015, had hardly showed any interest in responding to environmental issues. Nevertheless, the two main opposition parties, Liberal Party and New Democratic Party have shown public leadership on environmental issues, including climate change. This leadership, even though in opposition, may explain the continuing interest of the majority of surveyed people in Canada in getting better responses to environmental issues. Also, in 2015 the Liberal Party was elected to government, including polices to address environmental issues, including environmental concerns over the controversial Keystone oil pipeline, that connects Canada and the USA.

In Australia, how did the surveyed public define the term environment? In 2012 they mainly referred to natural descriptors, such as 'nature' and 'preservation', in line with the 1972 definition (10), see Table 3.1. In defining sustainability and sustainable living they used similar natural descriptors, like 'ecosystem' and 'alternative fuels'. Again, in this view the places for agriculture and industry in the global environment are absent.

Understanding the different views on environment

To bring down the environmental impasse it would be usefully first to deconstruct the views about environmental held by environmental supporters on one hand and agriculture, industry and government on the other, to show the values and limits of these attitudes, and then build up new attitudes to allow conversations across the current impasse, the new approach, discussed in Chapter 4.

Table 3.1 How the Australian public defined the terms 'environment' and 'sustainability'/'sustainable living' in the 2012 survey (20).

Term	Participant descriptors
'Environment'	Nature, Surroundings, Community, Green, Damage, Clean, Future/ Preservation, Resources, Cost/Reward/ Deterrent, Infrastructure.
'Sustainability'/ 'sustainable Living'	Ecosystem, Trees, Biodegradable, Re-using/recycle, Green environment. An environment that can persist. The ability of continued growth of life. Solar power, self sufficiency/self sustaining, affordable energy, Alternative fuels.

To better understand the different views across an impasse can improve respect for each stakeholder group, and so open further dialogue, with fewer and better disagreements (7). This approach has been utilised, for example, to improve the debate on global energy policy and genetically modified (GM) crops (26, 31).

To look at the attitudes of the different groups and to different sectors of society, we differentiated the perceptions of these by small and large scales of lifestyle, agriculture and industry sectors.

In the 1972 view, to reach a sustainable society Goldsmith and co-authors' proposal included, "Decentralization of polity, and economy at all levels and the formation of communities small enough to be reasonably self-regulating and self-supporting...." (10). This notion is a throwback to about the 17th century, with agrarian based economies and thus most people living in villages or small towns. At this time the world population was of only about 600 million, and at this population size the agrarian economies were reasonably successful. However, by July 2015 the growing world population had reached 7.35 billion (6). At this population size, and with the limited availability of unused land, it is clearly unreasonable to expect all people on earth to live in villages or small towns. Nevertheless, many environmental activists believe that optimally people should live in a village, with cottage industry and organic farming, corresponding to the small scale in Table 3.2. An example of such a lifestyle village is Nimbin, located in New South Wales, Australia. Also, in this view cities, living at large scale, are industrial manmade and unnatural.

In contrast, government and industry tend to see villages as inefficient, due to the higher costs of providing services compared to cities. Conversely these sectors see cities as having efficient economies of scale. In the new approach (Chapter 4) we see benefits to the natural and urban environment of high density living in cities.

Table 3.2 Perceptions of lifestyle at small and large scale.

	Scale	
Group/ era	Small	Large
20th C	Village^A	City
Environmental activists	Natural, environmentally friendly	Industrial, manmade, unnatural
Industry & Government	A valuable option in regional areas, though inefficient	Economies of scale
21st C	Regional option and Lifestyle choice. Include 'The Urban (Built) Environment'	Benefits to the environment of high density living^B. Include 'The Urban (Built) Environment'

A, Goldsmith et al. (1972) and others.
B, Can we really expect 8, 9 or 10 billion people to all live in villages for sustainable living?

For agriculture environmental activists see the small, single farmer, organic farm as natural and sustainable, while viewing large commercial farms as having opposite values, being unnatural and unsustainable, see Table 3.3. On the other hand, government and mainstream agriculture see organic farming as inefficient, while large commercial farms gain efficiency in part through economies of scale and are also improving land conservation, for example through the National Landcare Network in Australia (NLNA).

In the new approach (Chapter 4) we see the presence of similar ecosystems in both organic and large farms. At large scale benefits derive from building knowledge of ecosystems for introduced (non-native) crop plants, and considering agriculture systems as part of the earth's environment.

This approach is not to deny advantages of living at small scale, such as for reducing the distances food is transported from the time of its production until it reaches the consumer, a concept called 'Food Miles'. Food miles is one factor used when assessing the environmental impact of food, including the impact on global warming due to greenhouse emissions during transport and cool storage of food. So, as most people live in cities we may improve the environmental sensitivity and liveability of large scale city living by utilising concepts from living at small scale.

Although crops used for animal feed ultimately produce human food in the form of meat and dairy products, they do so with a substantial loss of caloric efficiency. On average, 10 g of vegetable protein are needed to generate 1 g of animal protein. Also, in terms of life cycle factors in producing foods, such as use of land, water and energy, non-vegetarian meals may have roughly a 1.5- to 2-fold higher factor than for vegetarian meals,

Table 3.3 Perceptions of agriculture at small and large scale.

Group/ era	Scale	
	Small	Large
20th C	Organic Farm[A]	Large Farm
Environmental activists	Natural, sustainable. Improving land conservation and animal handling.	Unnatural, unsustainable.
Government & Mainstream Agriculture	Inefficient (~2/3 of normal yield).	Efficient, economies of scale. Improving land conservation and animal handling.
21st C	Lifestyle choice. Building knowledge of ecosystems for introduced crop plants.	Building knowledge of ecosystems for introduced crop plants.
	To consider agriculture as part of the environment.	To consider agriculture as part of the environment.
Ecology	Ecosystems[B]	Ecosystems[B]

A, Goldsmith et al. (1972) and others.
B, Introduced species (indigenous plants in Australia have low food potential, see Chapter 5).

in which meat has been replaced by vegetable protein. Although on average vegetarian diets may well have an environmental advantage, exceptions may also occur. Long-distance air transport, deep-freezing, and some horticultural practices may lead to environmental burdens for vegetarian foods exceeding those for locally produced organic meat. (23).

For industrial manufacturing processes environmental activists prefer small-scale, such as the farmhouse for cheese making, which they see as a natural system. Elsewhere they see the large-scale cheese factory as industrial and unnatural, see Table 3.4. On the other hand, government and industry see the farmhouse as a small business with limited efficiency, and see large-scale cheese manufacturing as providing economies of scale, including financial income from exporting products. However, these groups also tend to see manufacturing as divorced from the natural environment.

In the new approach (chapter 4) we see benefits to the natural environment of large scale efficiency of manufacturing plants, which are supported by sustainable utilisation of resources. These companies will consider waste products as resources to be recycled and industry as part of the earth's environment.

Table 3.4 Perceptions of Industry at small and large scale. In this case cheese making in the dairy industry.

	Scale	
Group/ era	Small	Large
20th C	Farmhouse[A]	factory
Environmental activists	Natural	Industrial, unnatural.
Industry & Government	Small business, niche markets, limited efficiency.	Economies of scale, Processes divorced from the natural environment.
21st C	Local niche markets. Waste as resources. To consider industry as part of the environment.	Benefits to the environment of efficient, sustainable, large-scale industry. Waste as resources. To consider industry as part of the environment.
Ecology	ecosystem	ecosystem

A, Goldsmith et al. (1972) and others.

Conclusion

The observed decrease in public support of natural environments is consistent with the malaise in government leadership for responding to natural environmental issues.

The different attitudes from environmental activists and mainstream agriculture/industry and government to natural environments are consistent with the slow responses to natural environmental issues.

To gain faster responses to environmental issues we need environmental activists on one hand, and mainstream agriculture/ industry and government on the other to respect their different approaches to environmental conservation. To breakdown the impasse on improving responses to environmental issues requires improved mutual respect by the different groups.

It is also critical that mainstream agricultural and industrial companies become stakeholders for the natural environment. We discuss how to do this in the next chapter.

References

1. Callick, R. (2014) RBA member John Edwards argues it's time to move on from Hawke-Keating era. *The Australian*. http://www. theaustralian.com.au, accessed 26-5-14.

2. Carson, R. (2002) [1st. Pub. Houghton Mifflin, 1962]. *Silent Spring*. Mariner Books. ISBN 0-618-24906-0.

3. Cooper, T. (2016) British environmental history. Making history. http://www.history.ac.uk, accessed 27-4-16.

4. Courtney, P. (2000) Potter Plan revitalises farms. 20/02/2002, Landline, ABC Television. http://www.abc.net.au, accessed 9-1-17.

5. Crosby, A.W. (1986) *Ecological Imperialism: The Biological Expansion of Europe, 900-1900*. Cambridge University Press.

6. Department of Economic and Social Affairs, United Nations (2015a) *World Population Prospects: The 2015 Revision, Key Findings and Advance Tables*. Working Paper No. ESA/P/WP.241.

7. Fischhoff, B. (2013). The sciences of science communication. *PNAS.* 110 (Supplement 3): 14033-14039.

8. Flannery, T. (2010) *Here on Earth. An argument for hope.* Text Publishing, Melbourne, Australia.

9. Galbraith, J. K. (1992) *The Culture of Contentment.* Houghton Mifflin; First Edition. For a summary by J. K. Galbraith see: http://www.c-span.org/video/?33779-1/book-discussion-culture-contentment, accessed 22-10-14.

10. Goldsmith, E., Allen, R., Allaby, M., Davoll, J., and Lawrence, S. (1972) A Blueprint for survival. *The Ecologist,* 2(1): 1-22, and Penguin Books. http://www.theecologist.org/back_archive/19701999/, accessed 9-1-17.

11. Goldsmith, E. (1988). *The Great U-turn: de-industrializing society.* Green Books.

12. Hobbs, R.J., Higgs, E.S. and Hall, C. (editors) (2013) *Novel Ecosystems: Intervening in the New Ecological World Order.* John Wiley & Sons, Oxford. 380 pp. ISBN: 978-1-1183-5422-3.

13. Industry Skills Council (2009) Environmental Sustainability: An industry Response. (This discusses skills relating to sustainable practice). http://www.isc.org.au/pdf/FA_ISC_Sustainability_Report_Single_LR.pdf, accessed 9-4-13.

14. ISSP Environment I, II, III data analysis. Original responses to survey questions were generally collected in six groups; Very willing, Fairly willing, Neither willing or unwilling, Fairly unwilling, Very unwilling, Can't choose (Figure 3.1) or Agree strongly, Agree, Neither agree nor disagree, Disagree, Disagree strongly, Can't choose (Figure 3.2). To simplify presentation the responses were collected into three groups, as shown in the figure legends. Generally, there were no 'Can't choose' responses.

15. ISSP Research Group (1995) International Social Survey Programme: Environment I – ISSP 1993. GESIS Data Archive, Cologne. ZA2450 Data file Version 1.0.0, doi:10.4232/1.2450.

16. ISSP Research Group (2003) International Social Survey Pro-

gramme: Environment II – ISSP 2000. GESIS Data Archive, Cologne. ZA3440 Data file Version 1.0.0, doi:10.4232/1.3440.

17. Leopold , A. (1949) *Sand County Almanac: And Sketches Here and There*. Oxford University Press.

18. Lovelock, J.E. (1 August 1972) Gaia as seen through the atmosphere. *Atmospheric Environment* (1967) (Elsevier) 6(8): 579-580.

19. Lovelock, J.E., and Margulis, L. (1 February 1974) Atmospheric homeostasis by and for the biosphere: the Gaia hypothesis. *Tellus. Series A* (Stockholm: International Meteorological Institute) 26 (1–2): 2-10.

20. New South Wales Government (1994-2012) Who Cares about the Environment? New South Wales Government, Australia. http://www.environment.nsw.gov.au, accessed 5-1-17.

21. National Landcare Network, Australia. http://nln.org.au, accessed 9-10-14.

22. Marks, K. (2014) Australia scraps carbon tax: Tony Abbott makes his country a 'global pariah' after legislation is passed by Senate. *The Independent*, United Kingdom, 17 July 2014. http://www.independent.co.uk, accessed 16-10-14.

23. Reijnders, L. and Soret, S. (2003) Quantification of the environmental impact of different dietary protein choices. *American Journal of Clinical Nutrition*, 78(suppl): 664S–8S.

24. Siegel, M. (2014). Australian parliament repeals carbon tax, emissions trading scheme. 17-7-2014, Reuters. http://www.reuters.com, accessed 26-10-16.

25. Smith, D.F. (2000) *Natural Gain in the Grazing Lands of Southern Australia*. UNSW Press, Australia.

26. Sovacool, B.K., Brown, M.A., and Valentine, S.V. (2016) *Fact and Fiction in Global Energy Policy. Fifteen Contentious Questions*. Johns Hopkins University Press, USA.

27. Stutz, W.E. (2014) Repairing ecosystems. *Science*, 345: 388.

28. The Australian Industry Group (2007) Environmental Sustainability and Industry: Road to a sustainable future. (Findings of a national survey on environmental sustainable practices in industry) http://pdf.aigroup.asn.au, accessed 8-3-13.

29. Thoreau, H.D. (1854) *Walden; or, Life in the Woods*. Ticknor and Fields: Boston. http://thoreau.eserver.org/walden00.html, accessed 9-1-17.

30. Vala, J. and Ramos, A. (2014) International Social Survey Programme: Environment III – ISSP 2010 (Portugal). GESIS Data Archive, Cologne. ZA5516 Data file Version 1.0.0, doi:10.4232/1.11793.

31. Wolstenholme, J. (2016). Healing the rift around GM crops. British Ecological Society. http://www.britishecologicalsociety.org/healing-rift-around-gm-crops/, accessed 26-10-16.

4

NEW APPROACH TO ENVIRONMENTAL
MANAGEMENT

Here we show how a deeper knowledge and understanding of history can bring the managers of various ecosystems together and substantially improve environmental management.

New inclusive definition of the environment

For mainstream agricultural and industrial companies to become stakeholders (often joint) in conserving the natural environment we first need a definition of the earth's environments that is inclusive, rather than selective. We propose the definition;

> The environment is a system/collection of systems that includes all living organisms and the air, water, soil and buildings which is their habitat, including humans and our synthetic constructions.

In this way, we inclusively state that all human activities and the surface of rocks and soil and water around the planet comprise the earth's environments. In other words, it includes the natural environments; air, oceans, soil and groundwater, and those contrived and affected by humans; urban, agriculture and industry.

An urban environment, sometimes partly differentiated by being called the built environment, can be described as a building or (re)constructed area aimed to increase utility to the community and it's well-being. That is, through aesthetically planning and constructing, health improving, and compatible landscapes with living structures, such as roof-top gardens for growing food. Study of the built environment is often associated with human comfort, public health and well-being.

All environments whether natural, urban, agricultural or industrial should be managed with attention to efficiency of material use and sustainability.

Nature of human activity and our relationship to natural environments

Being human inherently means having an adaptive capacity, especially in relation to producing food, called Agriculture. Domestication of plants and animals was slowly increased, especially from at least 10,000 years ago, as a basis to form the first small stable communities. From this beginning human societies have developed and changed continually over time with ever new technology and ways to manage things. We have created agricultural and industrial systems to address our needs, and continue to adapt (see Chapters 5, 6).

Valuing the natural environment: ecosystem services

Ecosystems are clusters of organisms having complex interactions mostly living, sometimes imposed on non-living components, for instance base rocks, or water flow. These interactions mediate processes that achieve major transformations of resources, which include primary production (based on the capture of energy from the sun by plants and algae to produce complex organic compounds), soil formation by weathering and the incorporation of remains, and the cycling of water and nutrients in terrestrial and aquatic ecosystems. These primary services support three key secondary services; controls of ecosystems, production of goods and resources, and cultural settings for humans. Together these transformations support and enrich human life and in recognition of this have recently been called ecosystem services (3).

Controls of services that are provided by ecosystems, are extremely diverse and include the intercession of pollen spread on crops and regulation of pests and diseases sharing ecosystem outputs such as food, fuel and fibre. Other regulating services imposed by humans are microclimate management and hazard control.

Production services are manifested in the goods people obtain from ecosystems, such as food and fibre, fuel in the form of peat, biomass including wood fuel, and water from rivers, lakes and aquifers. Goods may be provided by intensively managed ecosystems, such as agricultural and aquaculture systems and plantation forests, or by natural or semi-natural ones, for example in the form of capturing wild fish and game and harvest of other wild foods – exemplified by human hunter/gathering.

Cultural services are derived from environmental settings where humans interact with each other and with nature and that give rise to cultural pleasures and goods and other benefits. In addition to their natural features, over millennia. such settings are modified with the outcomes of interactions between societies, cultures, technologies and ecosystems. These comprise an enormous range of so-called 'green' and 'blue' spaces, such as gardens, parks, rivers and lakes, the seashore and the wider countryside, including agricultural landscapes and wilderness areas.

The flora and fauna of natural lands – the organisms present – tend to be extremely diverse and may contribute to a wide range of ecosystem services. Agricultural lands tend to be managed for lower diversity but per unit area generally contribute much more food supply. Management of both sorts of lands sustainably depends on the same principles.

For the purposes of 'environmental accounting', ecosystem services have been distinguished further as those that can be turned directly into benefits (called 'final ecosystem services') and those that support other services (called 'intermediate ecosystem services'). While still far from perfect, these distinctions are increasingly gaining acceptance in assessment processes around the world. Environmental accounting is further discussed in Chapter 6.

Agriculture as part of the environment

Since crop plants were recognised from natural growth by selection thousands of years ago, humans have intervened in natural processes to increase yields. These interventions and changes in farming practice in more recent times have been supported by science and research, so developing impressive properties. For example, primitive wheat plants were first farmed about 9,000 years ago, in the Middle East. This first wheat was the product of cross fertilisation between three lines of the grass family. The earliest cultivated yields, were probably as little as 0.25 tonnes per hectare (though plots were much smaller than one hectare), and remained in that order for thousands of years. Formal wheat breeding began in the 19th century, when single line varieties were created through selection of seed from a single plant noted to have desired properties. Modern wheat breeding developed in the first years of the 20th century and was closely linked to the development of Mendelian genetics. As growers (in due course called farmers) selectively bred new strains, and adopted new practices and technologies, yields have increased dramatically. In Australia wheat became a crop in low rainfall areas so between 1861 and 1900 average yields of 0.59 tonnes/hectare were the normal. Between 1991 to 2011 average yields had increased to 1.7 tonnes/hectare (1). In contrast, over the same period in the UK, which has high inputs of fertiliser and rain, average yields were 7.7 tonnes/hectare (2). High tonnages depend on high rainfall or good irrigation. In drier regions, using large machinery and other low cost inputs, two tonnes/hectare can be very profitable. Put another way, a thousand years ago one seed was 'sown' and two harvested: today one seed yields fifty – and rising. A recent Australian project near Geelong in Victoria, sowing wheat into soils with fertility raised by clover ley farming, gave yields of around 10 tonnes per hectare, with one exceptional plot yeilding15 tonnes per hectare. Today, wheat is grown around the world and feeds billions of people and animals.

After all these changes, like many food crops, modern wheat can be described as a non-indigenous crop, wherever around the world they are grown. Combined with modern agricultural practices environmental activists have tended to see mainstream agriculture as not natural.

Nevertheless, to get the most from environmental management it is best to see farmed crops as part of the local environment linked to, and at times dependent on, the surrounding agricultural and natural environments. The environmental nature of agriculture is discussed further in Chapter 5.

Industry as part of the environment

Next we show how industrial companies are connected to natural environments. In general manufacturing and service companies are connected to natural environments, usually in indirectly ways. Companies are part of society and operate with informal agreement by the wider society. Similarly, companies are located in local environments which are part of the global environment. There remain fundamental reasons to improve responses to environmental problems, Chapter 2, and the majority of people still support conservation of natural environments, despite the fall off in support by some (Figure 3.2). As part of society companies are in good positions to support conservation of natural environments, through minimising their use of resources, such as energy and water, and recycling physical resources (Chapter 6).

In addition, biotechnology manufacturing companies may be directly connected to natural environmental resources. Biotechnology companies in general use biological resources that at some time originated from natural environments, so these companies can know the importance of natural resources.

What is the relationship of natural and biotechnology processes and ecosystems? Let us consider an apple tree growing in the wild, see left part of Figure 4.1. An apple falls to the ground and begins to be broken down by native microbes, bacteria and fungi, living on the ground. Fungi use sugars from the apple to produce energy, carbon dioxide and alcohol. Next, we look at a company using apples to make cider. Juice is extracted from apples and added to a tank, right part of Figure 4.1. The juice is heated to kill native microbes, then cooled, and commercial yeast and sugar are added. The yeast uses the apple and commercial sugar to make energy, carbon dioxide and alcohol. The natural and industrial scenarios are essentially similar in that in both cases fungi make energy from apple material for their own growth, and also produce carbon dioxide and alcohol. In the natural ecosystem the reactions continue until all organic material is assimilated by the bacteria and fungi, whereas at the cider factory the reaction is controlled and stopped to produce a stable product.

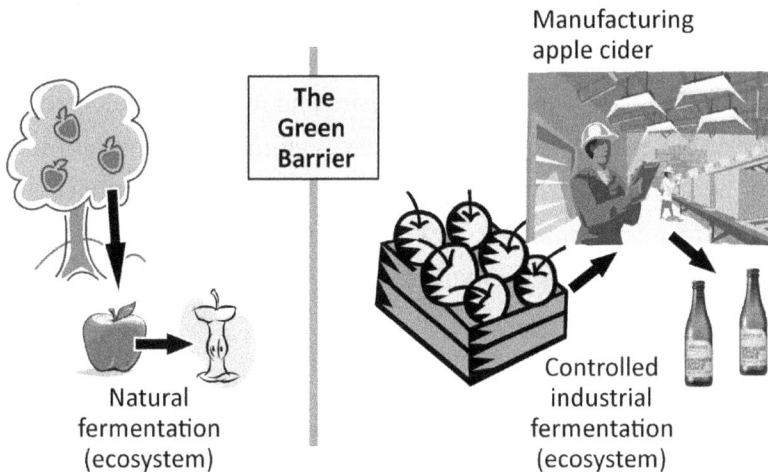

Figure 4.1. Fermenting apples: relationship of natural and industrial biotechnology ecosystems. Similar organisms and bioactivities may occur in both natural and industrial environments. Yeast microorganisms are involved in breaking down organic material, such as a fallen apple in a natural environment (left). Similar microorganisms are involved in controlled fermentation in industrial processes, such as manufacturing cider from apples (right). Also, organisms used by industry commonly have originated from natural environments. The Green Barrier bar symbolises the relative non-communication between natural fermentation scientists and industrial fermentation scientists, though knowing better of both systems would aid research on both sides.

Biotechnology industries include the Dairy, Food, Water and Pharmaceutical Industries. These industries may gain biological resources from natural environments and potentially improve their fermentation manufacturing processes, by (a) applying ecological scientific methods as well as chemical engineering methods to optimise fermentation processes, and (b) learning from natural fermentation ecosystems.

Fermented dairy foods include cheese and yoghurt, while in the main food industry fermented products include meats, like salami, and cider and wines from apples and grape varieties, respectively. In the water industry biological transformations are utilised to treat wastewater, increasing the total water available, and perhaps as importantly, to produce the solid component, called 'Biosolids', used as a fertiliser, and methane, collected as renewable energy. Also, in some cases animal feed and biofuels can be produced by algae grown in wastewater. Pharmaceutical companies search for new drugs from microorganisms and plants living in natural environments.

Externalities

An externality is a benefit (or cost) which results from an activity or transaction and which affects others. As an economic style concept this can be used to help industries to understand why they should be stakeholders for natural environments.

In this sense the activity is that industry will help maintain natural environmental resources and the resulting benefits are, (a) Direct: sustainably conserving resources required by industry, (b) Indirectly, to others: preserving quality of life for all humans, including our children and grandchildren, on planet earth, and (c) rehabilitation of sites used by industry but no longer needed, such as mines, for social purposes, such as parks or housing.

Conclusion

The new inclusive definition of environments is the basis for improving responses to environmental issues. This informs the relationships of natural, urban, agricultural and industrial environments in a clear and effective way. This also promotes a scientific evidence approach to sustainably operating agricultural systems (Chapter 5) and manufacturing and service companies (Chapter 6), as key parts of the global environment.

Including agriculture and industry as key parts of the global environment it will be easier to bring mainstream agricultural and industrial companies to become stakeholders for the natural environment.

This new inclusive way is to improve responses to environmental issues, and therefore sustainable life on planet earth for future generations, and applies to both developing and developed countries.

References

1. Australian Bureau of Statistics (2013) Historical Selected Agricultural Commodities, by State (1861 to Present), 2011. 71240DO001_201011. http://www.abs.gov.au, accessed 8-12-16.

2. FAOSTAT. Filters: production, crops. http://faostat3.fao.org/faostat-gateway/, accessed 9-10-14.

3. UK National Ecosystem Assessment (2011) The UK National Ecosystem Assessment: Synthesis of the Key Findings. UNEP-WCMC, Cambridge. http://uknea.unep-wcmc.org, accessed 24-6-14.

4. Smith D.F. and Hill D.M. (1975) Natural and agricultural ecosystems. *Journal of Environmental Quality*, June 1975, No 2.

5

AGRICULTURE AND THE NATURAL
ENVIRONMENT

Here we look at the substantial relationship between farming and the environment. Firstly, we examine the purpose of agriculture and, then, discuss agriculture as part of the environment, as a series of ecosystems.

The purpose of agriculture

The people must be fed! The people growing food commercially must get an adequate return, and the workers in the industry must be fairly treated. The productivity of the ecosystems must go on and on and on. There will be special ecosystems that can be called agriculture, in some form or other, producing food or fibre. The operators must heed any well-informed criticism from those from other callings, who care passionately about some particular aspects of the future of Planet Earth. At present many of these people believe agriculture/farming and conservation/caring for the environment are distinctly different activities, which are inevitably conflicting. Sometimes the basic cause is a deep objection to one in particular of the many activities, like the use of chemicals – using any is too much to some people. Sometimes the objection is broader. Far too frequently it is based on ignorance and/or misunderstandings of the processes of living things, or a refusal to accept reliable analysis and evidence.

Notwithstanding, agricultural and natural resource management have so much in common and are often inextricably intertwined so few causes could be more important than reconciling them.

We recognise agriculture as an ongoing mainstream activity of humans that is mostly grounded in sound ecological principles. Put simply, agriculture is a series of ecosystems resulting from millennia of adaptive human behaviour, in effect merging them through common processes. While it is mostly about producing human foods, it is sometimes associated with making clothing or shelter, and occasionally for production of fuels like ethanol.

How crops grow

Usually production of food crops involves using a plant growing with its leaves in the planet's atmosphere and with its roots in the soil, somehow, taking up some soil water with whatever happens to be dissolved in it. In the plant tops, the green leaves and stems, some of the water in vapour form is exchanged for carbon dioxide in the atmosphere. This process is making plant tissues, that is, growing, and also producing oxygen. This is concisely presented in Rain and Shine, a simple guide to how plants grow (23).

To survive long-term, the plant uses an interesting system: it flowers and generally mixes its genes with those of another of its species by accepting pollen, often in collaboration with insects, attracted by the flowers. Then it ripens a seed, which is genetically slightly different from either parent, and so may be able to adapt to slightly different environments – commonly that seed ends up somewhere else on soil. Humans have found that capturing some of this seed is a great way to feed themselves and sometimes they also use parts of the root system or the leaves. To gain more protein, they also bring other creatures into the system, including animals that eat parts of plants, most frequently the leaves. Humans then kill, cook and eat the animals so 'enriching' their diet with protein.

After the spark of life itself, the process in the green plant we call photosynthesis is the next greatest miracle on earth. It involves the capture of external energy from the sun and storing it as carbohydrates (CHOs), that is, sugar-like chemicals. In this process oxygen is produced, which is added to the atmosphere, thus making other life possible on the planet. In due course – sometimes a few hours, sometimes ages later – the stored CHOs are broken down, releasing the stored energy. Sometimes release is by digestion in living things, sometimes when dead matter is burned.

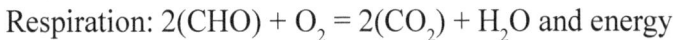

Photosynthesis: $CO_2 + H_2O + sun's E = CHO + O_2$

Respiration: $2(CHO) + O_2 = 2(CO_2) + H_2O$ and energy

The processes of crop growth involve many complex facets of science. One component is the set of biological cycles. There are perils for those who would intervene in these, for whatever reason. This chapter aims to widen understanding of the complexity and interrelatedness of agriculture and conservation and to shine a bright light on the conflicts, hopefully reducing them through better understanding. A fascinating underlying difference is between those who see the planet as organic – a natural order that comprises many, many cycles, feedback loops and balancing mechanisms yet not denying evolutionary change – and those who consider it much more of a machine with linear processes. The answer surely lies somewhere in between, it is a mixture of such elements, the living part more flexible than the linear processes. Agriculture is a mixture of cycles and one-way changes to generate produce, with the managers managing both as needed. They are generally more concerned with outcomes (mostly expressed as yields) rather than inputs, except where these are from external sources and have real costs. Nevertheless, soils must be recognised as providers of inputs and losses though leaching and erosion must also be considered.

Agriculture as part of the environment: ecosystems

Part of the problem to gain a better understanding of agriculture is the way in which any individual's knowledge is gathered. In education parts of the story 'reside' in different subjects taught by various teachers. These subjects are most often nowadays about aspects of an urban life, somewhat disconnected from land and agriculture. The basic life processes of photosynthesis and respiration are taught as part of biology. The wider sweep of organic chemistry is a specialised subject for science students. Learning about conditions in the atmosphere, climatology, nowadays has a heavy emphasis on climate change, so its possible impact is talked about in many subjects, but the fundamentals are rarely considered. The more recent subject environmental science ought to be a good source of understanding, though the tendency is to focus on the outcomes rather than the fundamentals. The subject agricultural science is, not unreasonably, taken by only a small minority of students. In total, it is just too easy to hear and learn only part of the story, with oversimplifications and risks of wrong-held conclusions.

Agriculture, however, as typical of ecosystems, often has high complexity. A great deal of it is to do with intricate natural events, with humans regulating them in time and intensity to make carefully defined outcomes, to maximise human benefit. As a simple comprehensible example, sheep left to roam freely may well have enough fodder most of the time, but for a few weeks in the year have some severe shortages. At such times overgrazing results and erosion and land degradation can occur. The ewes may mate and have lambs over much of the year. Many lambs are then lost to foxes or other predators and many sheep have worm infestations and diseases from time to time. Humans dependent on the sheep may not be able to plan the output, both for the family food and marketing to others, so having periods of inconvenience and income scarcity. Accordingly, instead of leaving the sheep to roam, farmers contain the animals with fencing, moving them to optimise pasture production and utilisation. They also grow more feed by using plant fertilisers and manage the time of mating and lambing to fit into seasons of peak plant production. In times of slow growth of forage, farmers have hay or grain to feed them. In addition, they protect sheep from predators and treat animals to prevent diseases. As a result, farming then provides a predictable supply of meat, both for 'home' consumption and, reliably, through 'markets', for people who do not have sheep. The sheep live longer and are healthier. The soil is less likely to be eroded.

The free-roaming and on-farm management set-ups could each be described as an animal/plant ecosystem. Clearly the latter could be managed to have a much less severe impact on the planet earth, while having a greater benefit for humans. Certainly, some of the actions in the system have scope to have unintended consequences beyond the system, such as fertilisers sometimes being washed into streams. So, what is important is the degree to which humans take complete responsibility with full supporting knowledge. In this chapter we suggest that the most important four-letter word in human management of ecosystems is to KNOW, to have the knowledge and to act accordingly.

Is there any simple basis on which to divide up ecosystems? Can we even distinguish agricultural-based and natural ecosystems? Some people would use concepts like intensity/amount of human management, biological diversity, or net energy balance to maintain the system. On 'amount of human management', just compare a public park, that is expected to be nice and green all year, and some sheep pastures. The park may need regular fertilising and watering and mowing and worn spots where too many people walk must be repaired, such as with instant lawn. Also, human rubbish must be taken away, regulations must be policed and dog poo taken away. By comparison some extensively grazed rangelands in low rainfall areas may only need the gate opened once a year to muster the animals, though in higher rainfall areas there is more intensive management, such as application of fertiliser and more grazing management. Is there greater biodiversity? Many grazing lands include hills and dales, deep soils and shallow soils, wet spots and dry spots and clusters of trees and woodlots. Collectively these generate a great range of habitats that may include untamed animals and birds, thus maintaining great biodiversity. By comparison, the public park may have very narrow biodiversity, though there are sometimes delightful inclusions of shrub clusters and flower beds. Then there is the extreme of crop land sown not only to one species, but also only to one genotype, while all others are excluded as far as possible. In this case there are serious issues with regard to the risk of failure in the growth of crops, so it is better to consider maintaining biodiversity over the landscape. We discuss this later.

Net energy balance is an interesting study, and we now know we must have solar input and include as much carbon sequestration as possible – pasture may be a great input pump. A vital piece of knowledge that many do not have is that carbon sequestration is in a compound with nitrogen, phosphorus and sulphur. Pasture would normally contain legumes which access free nitrogen from the atmosphere and farmers would likely make regular dressings of phosphorus fertiliser that contains sulphur from the manufacturing process. The public park may well be a huge sink for energy but have poor capacity to sequestrate carbon. Nevertheless, the clippings are a store of carbon so can be used. Clearly there can be endless debate about exercises like this, and huge variation within categories, but this exercise is fruitful in illustrating similarities and differences. Further, there are features of some natural systems that are dear to the heart of conservationists but of little consequence to mainstream farmers.

One who has contributed to the debate on such things is the American journalist Michael Pollan, who has asserted that there are key issues with the export of cheaply produced corn to Mexico under the free trade agreement (16). As a result, small Mexican farmers were being driven out of business and this would both reduce biodiversity and imperil the survival of different variant crops' genes. In relation to this the International Maize and Wheat Improvement Center (CIMMYT) was established in the middle of last century, with its head quarter located in Mexico, as one of a chain of international stations. Among other things, CIMMYT was charged with maintaining the corn gene bank because the survival of these genes is too important to be left to the vagaries of weather and the behaviour of small-area farmers.

Finally, there is another matter to keep in mind: who pays the piper? What is not widely enough recognised is that sustaining the ability of the ecosystems to produce things is inherently more important in farming areas than the 'outputs' of non-farmed reservations. The people managing the farm land must gain an adequate income through managing to produce crops and animals over the long-term, and they will aim to pass on the land to their children or shareholders in a productive state. In contrast, the incomes of managers for conservation areas are paid from the public purse as are all costs of inputs. Also, sustainable management of both farms and parks are susceptible to short-term solutions by economic difficulties or government cut-backs.

Some illustrative scenarios

It is useful to look at a sample of the ecosystems that have evolved, from the 'beginning', when *Homo sp* became humans rather than simply behaving as just another creature. As these are described, adaptive behaviour will be identified – and sometimes lack of it. The examples come from various times in history and from all continents, with Australia, being such an interesting case, having some prominence.

There are some adjectives that are commonly (mis)used and can lead us astray. In many parts of the world, such as in central Africa, the word traditional is used to describe the agriculture, with claims that activities derived some time ago and proven by time to be good responses to that environment are the best to fill needs of the people. It is implied that the systems are intrinsically good and must remain the same, continuing unchanged. Is this so?

In developed countries the related term 'conventional' is sometimes used to describe large scale mainstream farming. However, over the last 50 to 100 years management has been increasingly informed by observation and measurement, using crop growth models for guidance, rather than working to a set of conventions. Then practice is altered by adaptive behaviour. Obvious examples are the abandonment of tillage in preparation for cropping, 'new' irrigation systems based on laser-guided grading of the land and water applied in response to soil moisture measurement; growing fruit trees as trellises and hedge rows to better capture sunlight and harvesting fruit when the sugar content is just right; tagging animals with microchips so they can easily be weighed and given the right amount of feed and even moved on when measured residual pasture drops to a certain level. Thus, conventional is not a suitable adjective.

Australia is of special interest because settlement occurred very recently in the history of humans on the planet with two sets of arrivals: only 40 to 50,000 years apart; Aboriginals from islands to the north, arrived about 50,000 years ago, and Europeans in 1788. The latter developed widespread agriculture, including rain-fed agriculture in the semi-arid zone, out to the arid boundary, which is different in Australia than in any other continent, because of the shape of the continent. This development occurred late enough in the 19th century to utilise the fruits of human endeavours including scientific research and development and mechanisation, plant breeding, structures for domestic water supplies, railways, and even the use of aircraft. The areas on which irrigation was tried were the natural flood plains of the modest river systems, late enough to have mechanisation and now using laser beams to control mechanical equipment to provide perfect field gradients. Over the last few decades producing more output with less and less water has been a common management achievement. The results are irrigated farming ecosystems, which are significantly different from the ancient ones of the Middle East and Asia, and not in any sense conventional. All agriculture was assisted by the importation of plant varieties from the rest of the world and programs of breeding with plant material from other parts.

One could consider creatures being called humans once they exhibited communication by language, thinking, knowing and remembering, as part of their capabilities. This would be especially so in facing the things that would be important in their simple life: getting enough food through the various seasons, finding shelter from heat and cold, and having protection from predators and hazards, like wild animals and flood and fire.

Though marked as thinkers, it seems a fair assumption that early mankind would not have philosophy like considering 'The natural order of things must not be changed'. For them the simple criterion for commending a small change to the natural order would be that it seemed useful and made life easier and more pleasant. Their behaviour would be adaptive: small changes would follow from observing and testing. Gradually these have been more and more sweeping, and some would say savage, interventions. As with many other fields of human endeavour there was quite recently – in the last 500 years – a 'meeting' with science and technology, so agriculture became at the same time a user and a source of scientific information and technologies.

The scenarios will thus include a 'beginning' then some stops on the long journey through to present-day best-practice agriculture. Note must be taken of the important things that virtually define humans: **Thinking**, building up **The Body of Knowledge**, and examples of **Adaptive Behaviour**.

Beginnings of agriculture

Up to a certain point in history there would only have been creatures gently imposing themselves on natural ecosystems, taking what occurred naturally with little interference to influence the outcome, especially not to control 'yield'. Perhaps a good starting point for this discussion, is the broadly defined stage at which humans became humans, for example, hunter-gatherers living in a cave. They adapted to use a naturally occurring shelter, the cave, rather than use materials from the ecosystems to make one, such as, later wurleys, huts and houses. From these bases they gathered things from natural ecosystems for their food, and were likely to have had two sources, plants and animals. Plant material was mostly gathered by the females, who we call women from here on, and animal flesh obtained from hunting by the males, who we now call men. From our perceptions today, hunting, the men's activity, seems more exciting, but it would have been less reliable.

The women would aim to provide enough food for the children at all times, which was not always easy. One imagines a cave-woman would generally become familiar with the 'ecosystems' – the land and its plants and small creatures – in reasonable proximity to the cave. She would know what fruit, seeds, roots etc. were present. One can imagine such a woman one day exploring further from the cave, down the valley, perhaps because it was a nice day, perhaps because all the territory near the cave had been 'picked over'. She sees a tree with ripe fruit and samples it: it tastes better than any near 'home'. She takes some fruit home and when the fruit is eaten and being a human thinker decides to keep the seed and grow trees nearer home. In the next day or two she chooses a less dense spot in the vegetation near the cave, and with her digging stick opens up a narrow trench and buries several seeds. Overall her thinking is: this will mean less walking to pick the fruit in a few years-time and that she will be able to 'protect' it. By planting several seeds she is more certain to get at least one tree. While growing up she had been taught by her mother that it is better not to just drop faeces and urine on the cave floor, like animals do, and there could also have been a growing realisation that putting these wastes near plants seems to makes them grow better – some knowledge.

The following year she is pleased when most of the seeds germinate and she watches the trees grow. One wonders when it dawned on humans that rain falling on the soil and sunshine falling on foliage were good for growth. Let in rain, let in shine! If at some stage she realised that her new young trees were shaded by branches of existing trees, she would have broken off the offending branches. In due course the trees would have borne fruit. Is this the beginning of horticulture? Basically, a modern person is involved in the same activities as her cave-based ancestor, in selecting plant material of superior value, selecting a site in which to grow new plants, preparing the soil, reducing competition, and adding nutrients. All these are done with the aim of greater convenience and increased yield of nicer fruit – in our time with more sophisticated equipment!

A recent report on excavations in Northern Italy suggested the Neanderthal people were 'cave-proud', with sleeping areas separate from food areas (25). As a result they had less risk of getting up in the night and tripping over an animal's carcass. They prepared meals at the mouth of the cave, and had the fire at the back for more efficient heating, though surely a challenge with smoke and firewood management?

With regard to the men hunting animals, attempting to find animals roaming widely and getting close enough to hit one with a club sounds like fun to present day people in Four Wheel Drive vehicles, but could have been a tough task for early men on foot with crude clubs. Without much in the way of tools to trim wood, even a simple thing like making a good club would be a challenge. The idea of the spear was a real deep thinking brainwave, to find some special plant with tough, straight, flexible branches that could be cut with a stone axe, and could be fired to make the tip hard to form a good spear. Then, what is called butchering: cutting or tearing up the kill, would be a challenge as there were no metal knives until the last few thousand years. Getting the meat back to the cave and storing a portion of it so the kill lasts a few days longer, would be another challenge.

The men must have longed for some way of keeping some animals conveniently close ready to kill. Eventually they made an enclosure, using rocks or timber, which must have been hard work. What has been called domestication must have helped control animals. For instance, domesticating sheep was used to make them tame creatures, that weren't too aggressive, were of moderate size, easily shepherded and could be taken into the folds for protection against predators each night. The invention of wire in the last two hundred years was an incredible leap. Imagine farm life without the 'farmers' friend' as it is called in the country!

Much has been written about the development of farming, especially crop growing, using many seeds in the one area. It is not difficult to imagine gatherers setting aside some of the seed heads picked for food and 'planting' them, as did our cave woman above, and establishing an annual routine. They also naturally recognised superior sites, which had deeper soil that perhaps was also perceived as richer. Apparently this was just scattering of seed and what emerged when the rains came was a mixture of plants from the added seed and plants already growing on the site. Surely plants of little use, which have long been called weeds, would not have been welcome. Though some suggest that early humans did not have monoculture crops one suspects it was because it was just about impossible to remove all other, unwanted, plants. Modern research shows that monoculture crops normally give the best returns, though there are exceptions, like the deliberate inclusion of nitrogen fixing legumes, or use of shade trees. The big question was: How could unwanted plants, which clearly reduced the growth of the desired crop, be controlled? Mostly it had to be attempted by good old-fashioned, tedious hand weeding, which is fine on small areas. Eventually crude hoes were invented, and women had more work in swinging a heavy cast-iron hoe. These heavy hoes have persisted in parts of Africa under the guise of tradition! In many places 'technology' was used to reduce the work required by farmers.

In gaining an understanding of the adaptive behaviour and management of ecosystems for human benefit, time and place do not greatly matter. There were probably long periods of little change, then bursts of activity, such as about 12,000 years ago, when the current warmer period began in what is known as the Holocene geological period. Many of what are now called the climatic zones on the earth's surface were more or less established then, with more settled living, cultivating crops, learning to manage some animals, and even to shape metals and clays to make implements and aides. We have suggested even our cave woman recognised human waste could improve the growth of plants – the first fertiliser. Once farmers could produce surplus foods beyond their own requirements more people could be settled in one place, to form the beginning of villages and, eventually, towns and cities. Food could be produced at sites with better soil or water availability, but wastes could not easily be returned to the fields, especially when large cities developed. It is interesting to ponder when there was sharp recognition that separating human wastes from production areas increased depleting of soils. It is an odd paradox that these towns and cities almost inevitably reduced the fertile land available, a serious problem also in our time.

This leads into areas of huge disputation: drainage water capture and re-use. Another thing recognised was the carriage of disease by human excreta and urine entering water supplies. In some areas, such as Europe and Australia, people considered the risk of diseases carried by human waste too great to use sewage as fertiliser or effluent as irrigation water. This meant that the explosion in water 'needs' by cities was met by building vast dams, inundating pristine valleys, so fresh water could be used. In more recent times the efficacy of treatment is such as to consider wider re-use, especially for crop irrigation, applying the water underground and/or avoiding use on such things as salad vegetables. Notwithstanding, some experts warn that, with large city conurbations, a breakdown of treatment may have massive consequences.

Slash and burn farming was an early 'system', widespread in tropical and semi tropical forest areas in South and Central America and Central Africa. Low forest cover was cut down with slasher tools, allowed to dry, then burned, which released some nutrients and killed some residual plants. The land was then crudely cultivated with hand tools and seeds of a crop plant were scattered. Though the peasants consumed the crop harvest, it was very unlikely that the human wastes would be returned fully and evenly to the crop land. Though there was sometimes a small, slow release of some nutrients from the parent rock material, soil fertility generally declined, and crop yields fell. A fresh area was then used. With a small population and plenty of new land, the system was probably completely sustainable, and prevailed for thousands of years. Obviously there could be quite a range of cycle lengths: the higher the initial soil fertility, the more crops could be taken; where rock was being broken down more quickly, the more or better crops could be taken; where there were some other residues added, including human wastes, more or better crops could also be taken. This is essentially the organic farming opportunity: to settle on the soils with highest natural fertility, and have access to other residues such as manure from farm animals in winter keep, or hens in cages. In this case the system might operate for a long time. In a modern properly developed system what is removed is known and replaced in the most efficacious way: in terms of nutrient requirements, it is likely to be concentrated fertiliser.

There are still many parts of Africa where cropping is little changed from 1000 years ago, and it is rather unrewarding: soil fertility is run down, there are plenty of unwanted plants and heavy cast-iron hoes are still the main tool for all tillage/soil preparation, which demands much human effort. Perhaps most striking is that the women have taken over responsibility for most of the crop work, though it tends to swing back to the men if there is any mechanisation! But most of all there has been inadequate thinking, and disregard for the importance of knowledge not only by the locals, but, inexcusably, by other people arriving over the last few hundred years, who presumed to help.

One ponders the arrival of missionaries and what the locals made of their hymn using farming as a metaphor for spreading the Word of God (13):

We plough the fields, and scatter the good seed on the land.
But it is fed and watered by God's almighty hand ...

In modern times we would counsel that scattering seed is demonstrably foolish. It should be planted at the best depth and spacing. And, not to be offensive, one should leave God out of this: be personally responsible.

And then a Biblical parable (4):

A sower went out to sow ... some seed fell along the path, and the birds came and devoured it. Other seed fell on rocky ground ... Other seed fell among thorns and the thorns grew up and choked it and it yielded no grain. And other seeds fell into good soil and brought forth grain ... yielding thirtyfold and sixtyfold and a hundredfold.

Surely, don't waste good seed on poor ground; perhaps tie up the goats there to improve it. Also, remove competing thorns and weeds. Finally, think and analyse: why did that crop yield a hundredfold, and aim for that every time. In this way the farmer can maximise return from both the woman's labour and the land. There must be precise sowing, at best depth, spacing along the row and between rows to optimise the capture of the sun's energy.

In developed countries crop production tends to be part of a system that integrates human skills, with different tools and timing, comprising a number of activities. In Africa there is often no such integration. A system typically includes more than one person working at separate times using tools specific to the task. It might be improved by the following:

Day 1: One woman moves along the rows with a light-weight, long-handled, wide-bladed, sharp hoe slicing off the weeds just below ground level. As damage is common, she is told to keep well clear of the crop plants. She works till mid-afternoon, at the latest, to cut and displace weeds, as these will die better while the sun is on them. She goes home, has a rest, then prepares for the children to come from school. In many situations she should put 'Crocs', cheap plastic sandals, on their feet as they go out to play, to reduce the chance of infection by hookworm and the worm that causes river-blindness. She has the energy to prepare a good meal and supervise any school homework.

Day 3: Another woman works through the crop hoed on day 1. Her task is to 'kill' any weeds from the day 1 cultivation that have not wilted/died and to remove the weeds near the crop plants, taking care not to damage any. She works from a light kneeler made from Eucalypt timber, using a combination of good old-fashioned hand weeding and a light-weight 'tickle' hoe. She may finish even earlier in the day.

Fertiliser: The kneeler may include a holder for critical phosphatic fertiliser. For spaced crops she may add a bottle top full to each plant or spread if in rows.

In some cases there could be legumes in rotation or alternate rows, which are fixing atmospheric nitrogen. It is not hard to imagine doubling of yields. Why has there not been more thinking in this matter? Surely improved hoes should long have been a target for Aid Agencies.

Sadly, for several centuries missionaries and aid agencies have been blind to the effects of low yields on women and, therefore, family life. Also, there has been emphasis on adoption of expensive mechanisation – what about the possibilities of improvement without it? Early humans can be forgiven as they lacked knowledge, but in modern times, in the face of current knowledge, such behaviour is unforgiveable. In many areas, soil fertility has declined and degradation increased. Organic production will only succeed if nutrient rich materials are available, as is often the case in Europe from winter keep and intensive animal production units, but very rarely in Africa. Judicious use of mineral fertilisers is essential, especially phosphorus, and even some nitrogen while legume based systems are being developed.

To sum up, the system must involve building on the way our early seed collectors worked to seven steps: 1) use quality selected seed; 2) include legumes so crops have plenty of nitrogen; 3) complete weed removal; 4) add small doses of critical plant nutrients – a supply chain for this is a priority; 5) tie up the goats; 6) harvest at the best time; and 7) ensure safe storage of harvested foods. The importance of maximising yield can be seen from data giving reduced acres of land planted per person of population on the planet: 1950: 0.24 acres per person, 1986: 0.15 acres, 2000: 0.12 acres.

The Aboriginals were apparently the first humans to settle on the Australian land mass. Until then the land was *terra nullis*, unoccupied by humans. This was quite remarkable given many ages of human evolution elsewhere, but it meant the new arrivals were on their own. There was no earlier activity to build on or people from whom to learn about the peculiar flora and fauna. It is commonly assumed that these Aboriginals were hunter-gatherers, inferring they did not do anything resembling farming. However, it is known that early Aboriginals farmed kangaroo grass, and milled the grain to make flour, which could be used for making food and stored for future use (15).

The continent was largely semi-arid with plains and rangelands carrying shrubs. The coastal fringe had better rainfall, especially across the south, with better winter seasonal rainfall. There were various plants that had edible roots or fruits, though rather scanty in parts. Travelling to this continent in their small boats, the people apparently brought no animals larger than dogs, so their traditional knowledge of animals, such as fore-runners of goats and sheep, would not have had any value. New to them were birds, snakes and lizards, and a lot of strange animals that hopped – kangaroos and wallabies.

The kangaroo was potentially the most useful meat animal, though catching it would obviously have been a challenge with its long leap and hopping speed. But being humans – adaptive, thinking people – they worked out management systems. The main one involved use of fire, burning the dry grass near certain water holes with several effects. Firstly, when it rained any green shoots of regrowth plants would be visible and attractive to the kangaroos, increasing the chances that the kangaroos and other game would come to their water hole. Here the hunters would arrange 'hides' to get close to them. Secondly, the burning would also have recycled nutrients from the dry grass and plant debris, so stimulating plant regrowth, though they would not have known it, nor would they have recognised that this depleted the soil organic matter and made some soils more prone to erosion.

Should their system based on generation of better green grass around water holes be called hunting? They apparently spared females, especially those with visible joeys in their pouches. So, should this be called animal husbandry? At rivers they set eel traps. Is it fair to absolutely classify them as hunter-gatherers? Their efforts near the water holes could easily be described as a form of livestock farming.

The climate of much of Australia is temperate but these people needed shelter at times, and were frequently on the move, being nomadic. Thus, they constructed shelters, called wurleys, which were made of tree branches. Wurleys were fairly quickly built and readily abandoned. Caves were not common in the Australian landscape.

The Europeans, arriving in Australia a little more than 200 years ago, brought animals and plants from Europe. Some of the settlers grazed sheep on the same ecosystems as those on which the Aborigines had taken kangaroos, again using the water supply points. Evolving through use of windmills and solar powered pumps, modern water supply systems are often very sophisticated. They are now fenced well enough to exclude all animals, including feral camels and horses. The access gate, controlled by a computer, is opened when a camera 'sees' the image of sheep or cattle: whatever is selected. Thus, only selected animals are allowed in to drink. Individual sheep and cattle usually carry an Identification (ID) chip that can be read by an electronic sensor, so survival can be recorded. Through use of the camera an assessment of the animal's condition can even be made. The site can be far away from human habitation. It is not hard to see the possibilities for precise animal grazing. This meshing of wire, energy and computer technologies is a crowning 'glory'. It goes part way to dealing with the very large problem of the adaptation of animals from other lands to the Australian rangeland ecosystem. Horses, camels, goats and pigs, all have joined in and sought a place. Culling of feral animals is essential, though animal cruelty is a challenge: if a poor shot taken from the helicopter wounds an animal, the operator must loop back to ensure a kill.

The sheep-for-lamb-meat industry of Iceland is another example of intelligent ecosystem management. The basic animal unit is an ewe whose DNA has been checked for genes for triple ovulation, so producing three lambs – triplets. These ewes pass the cold snowy winter in special enclosures in hillsides, which are rather cave-like, thus conserving body heat. There is just room for ewes to reach feed and to mate. Lambing is planned to coincide with spring and the burst of pasture growth. The ewe produces three lambs so there are four sheep to graze on the prolific spring and summer pastures. Some surplus pasture is made into high grade hay and silage to feed the ewes during the next winter. As the autumn falls the lambs are ready to sell into the meat markets of Europe. This is an excellent example of modern farming involving modelling of the enterprises and precise timing of events like lambing and growth of animals to market weight.

In Western countries there was quite a lot of low input farming, including several domesticated animals, confined in various ways, bringing animals and a range of plants together on one site, called a mixed farm. Using the broad skills and labour of the farmer and his family such units can be almost totally self-sufficient, sometimes with small surpluses of various products to market for cash. One example was Benmore Farm, at Green Hills south of Adelaide in South Australia. In the depression years 1920s and 1930s this was the home of the Smith family, parents and four children, including David Smith, one of the authors of this book.

This farm was on a ridge high enough to receive good rainfall, about 750 mm per annum. Part of it was natural grassland with scattered eucalypt trees, and it ran about 10 dairy cows. These were milked by hand, and the cream separated from the milk using a hand operated centrifuge. The cream was sold to a local butter factory and the skim milk was fed to piglets and calves, the latter sold for meat at a few months of age if males, kept as replacement cows if female. Much of the farm was scrub-land, with trees that could be cut for fence posts and rough timber, and the debris burned and crops grown. Wheat had been grown by earlier settlers but winter rainfall was too high for that crop and, in any case, the ancient landscape had long been leached of vital plant nutrients like phosphorus and potassium and molybdenum. However, knowledge was awakening about plant nutrition (molybdenum used nearby, the first in the world!), so the crops of Brussel sprouts and potatoes and turnips were given dressings of blood and bone fertiliser, a bi-product of the nearby abattoirs for providing meat for Adelaide city. The surplus vegetable produce was sold in the Adelaide City Market, to bring in a small income. For the family there was a 'kitchen' vegetable garden with every possible vegetable, including peas, beans, lettuces, cauliflowers, cabbages, carrots and turnips. Fruits grown were gooseberries, quinces, apples and plums. Birds ate much of the fruit. Blackberries were picked from wild brambles.

A pig yard and sty had been constructed from some logs split with a maul and wedges: no saw. Four sows and a boar were usually kept and the young pigs eaten, some marketed. A poultry run was made with some difficulty, as wire mesh cost money. It was not fox proof, so the hens were shut in a small shed every night: occasional neglect wrought awful losses. The eggs were laid wherever a hen made a nest, so seek and ye shall find. Feral rabbits bred freely in the scrub and consumed a lot of pasture, but the children trapped and dug them out, so rabbit was a main meat dish and was cooked various ways, alternating with pig meat and poultry. A rare treat was sausages bought from a passing butcher. With no refrigeration, meat was often 'off' in more ways than one.

There were two horses to pull the implements, the ploughs, harrows and sledges. Horse-drawn sledges were the main means of transport on steep hills, safer than a wheeled dray. A six-seater horse drawn trap was used to visit the small town 5 km away. In the house lighting was by kerosene lamp and heating by wood fires, an open hearth and a metal stove. The water supply was roof water caught in tanks and moved about by bucket, except for the laundry/bathroom that was adjacent to the tank so it had a tap inside. Laundry and bathroom water was heated in a copper and moved about in a metal dipper.

As can be imagined, running such a labour-intensive farm based on natural ecosystems was a challenge, especially seizing the opportunity to gain some income from so many possibilities: for example, cream, calves, piglets, vegetables, wattle tree bark for a tannery, and rabbit skins. There were so many disappointments. Paradoxically, continuing the education of the older, stronger and more useful children deprived their availability for working at the farm, though keeping them at home to work deprived older children of life opportunities. The dependence of poor farmers on their children as farm workers remains an issue in many developing countries.

Versions of this mixed farm system have become popular in recent times, albeit with the disadvantages masked by separate income. One example, somewhat modernised, is the Polyface Farm in Virginia, USA, described in Michael Pollan's book, *Omnivore's Dilemma* (17). It too has a range of activities: hogs/pigs, cows, rabbits, potatoes, fruit trees, vegetables. Hens lay in mobile nests, much the same as the old seek and ye shall find. A truck is an improvement over the wheel barrow to cart the pig and cow manure to the vegetable garden, though it uses fossil fuel. There is often electricity to power many handy gadgets. Pollan suggests all of the creatures lead 'fulfilling lives', and there is nice 'ecological sculpturing' of the landscape, presumably including small dams and the like.

Some people hanker for something rather similar making much of local production/local consumption and internal interactions and suggest it is a glimpse of what may be in store for us over the course of the 21st century (9, 11, 17). Others suggest it is a great delusion, that such places are often a delusion for some members of affluent communities might indulge in and some poor people might be forced to use something like it. In reality a huge proportion of the world's population will live in compressed cities at some distance from farming areas. Most food will inevitably be produced some distance away by a farmer who is a product specialist, who maximises yield and return from inputs like land and energy and, increasingly, will contribute to effective carbon sequestration. Diversity will occur across the larger landscape, rather than on a local farm scale. All of this and the 'food miles' campaign is complex territory because food is often provided most efficiently through consideration of several equations that integrate production and transport efficiency and climatic suitability. As a result, food is produced and moved from paddock to plate with minimal energy and cost. The total flux of energy in these situations makes for fascinating studies.

On the other hand, there may be niches, as to feed the world will also require variability in diets, and special local supplies of seasonally available foods may have a place – at a price!

Evolution of precision farming

Australia provides an interesting study as mainstream large-scale cereal cropping was developed so late in human history. Initially this involved sharing knowledge and technologies from Europe. However, it was soon recognised that the local ecosystems had very different characteristics than the long settled European lands, so the settlers had to be very adaptive. Large areas of land had modest rainfall and attempts were made to grow cereal crops, especially wheat, on these lands rather than in higher rainfall areas. Recent crop history is most instructive in studying the interaction of agriculture and conservation.

The evolution of wheat farming in southern Australia is illustrated in Figure 5.1, which shows the changes in yields over time. This data is derived from work by Dr D. J. Connor and colleagues, from a collection of data for annual yield (5). Its beginning period, Phase I, has much in common with the slash and burn farming described above, except that the horse as a power source was widely available. Special equipment was made of iron: the blacksmith and ironmonger were important people. The native vegetation often included a small Eucalypt tree, which had a large stump and several stems. The stems were broken by dragging a log with horses pulling the ends, but the stumps were a problem. Then a clever plough was invented, the 'stump-jump plough': the tilling piece simply swung up, over and dropped down in front of the stumps, which were gradually removed over several years. It meant that land could be cropped for a financial return before all of the Mallee scrub tree roots had been removed. Soil preparation for sowing a crop could involve six to eight passes with horse-drawn tilling equipment and there was some pride in making the soil look like the home garden, a good seed bed. Notwithstanding, yields fell steadily, being calamitously low in the drier years.

After about 1900 Phase II followed, characterised by the introduction of bare fallowing. The field was kept free of all growth by cultivation as needed for a period of up to a year, then a crop sown. There were immediate and dramatic yield increases, especially as it coincided with the arrival of knowledge that the addition of phosphatic fertilisers could be beneficial. Also, new varieties were extensively especially bred for the conditions, particularly by William Farrer. He was a very important migrant, who had first studied medical science in England. When he contracted tuberculosis he decided to move to Australia and live with some relatives on their New South Wales farm, as it

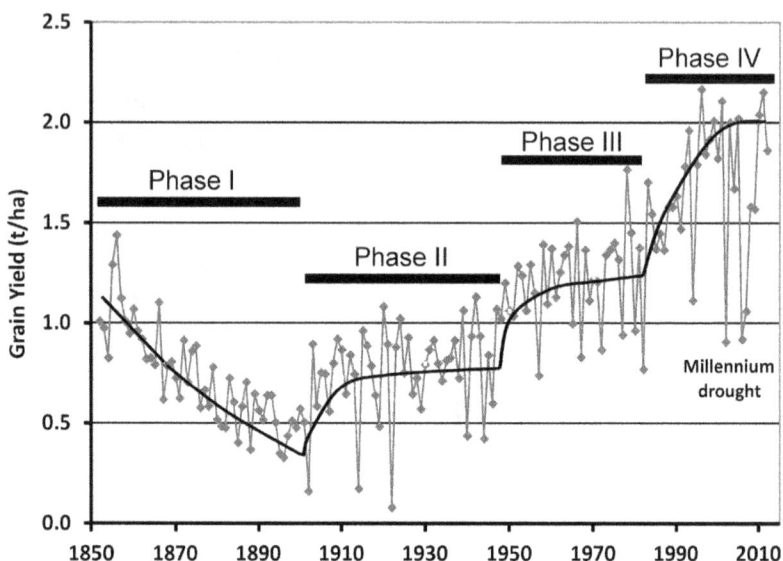

Figure 5.1. Changes in wheat yields in Australia during the period 1851 to 2012, over four phases. Diamonds mark individual year average wheat yields, black line shows trends. Yields tended to increase following agricultural adaptations over this time. Adaptation phases: Phase I, Clearing native plants to provide space for continual farming (1850-1900); Phase II, fallowing, using P fertilizer and new adapted wheat varieties (1901-1946); Phase III, mechanization of farm operations, use of legume pastures and herbicides (1947-1982); Phase IV, use of new semi-dwarf varieties of wheat plants and N fertilizers (1983-present). To feed our continually growing world population increases in yields must continue to occur in the future, along with reallocation of land for agriculture.

was thought that the warmer dryer climate there might cure the disease. When cured he worked as a breeder of wheat varieties for the new lands, and matched genotypes to ecological regions. He was brilliantly successful in breeding disease resistance and adaptability to the wide range of semi-arid lands. His influence on the growing nation cannot be overstressed and he has been called 'the father of the Australian wheat industry'.

Though the farmers didn't recognise it, unfortunately, the effect of tillage to keep the soil free of weeds was a mixture of good and bad. Aerating of the soil by the tilling promoted break down of soil organic matter, thus making nitrogen available, so increasing crop yields. Aeration also broke down soil organic matter, so carbon was also lost from the soil, in the form of carbon dioxide, to be emitted into the atmosphere. The breaking down of organic matter spoiled the structure of the soil, making it more easily eroded, and after heavy rains crusts formed on top. The temporary increases in crop yields meant this system was a real trap for the ignorant, as so often is the case until research scientists explain things. Time makes ancient good farmers appear uncouth!

Phase III was especially interesting in ecosystem change, primarily with the addition of specific auxiliary plants to fix nitrogen. As is occasionally the way with human endeavours, several technologies came together to dramatically change the scene. Firstly, about this time the legume – and therefore nitrogen fixer – subterranean clover, a plant migrant from southern Europe, came to be widely used on acid soils and the medics, also legumes, were grown on alkaline soils. Both legumes were grown in rotations with the cereals. Soon there was no need to fallow soil to release nitrogen, as an abundance was fixed from the atmosphere by the legumes. Secondly, an important piece of specific knowledge was that phosphorus is a vital element in chlorophyll, the key biochemical in the photosynthetic process in green plants and also an essential ingredient in sequestering carbon in the soil. Thus, the addition phosphatic fertiliser became routine and there were huge gains in plant herbage production, for both the crop and the pastures containing legumes.

A popular system was alternating periods of pasture, for example six years, and periods of cropping, such as four years. Under this, there was a long term upward trend in soil fertility – the level of carbon and nitrogen in the soil, and crop yields, were increased. This strongly regenerative system was called ley farming, and virtually banished soil erosion. This phase also coincided with the almost total mechanisation of crop growing in Australia, which replaced the work done by horses. However, the associated use of fossil fuels meant farmers became involved in the greenhouse gas debate, as well as issues around soil carbon.

Phase IV could be called The Present. Firstly, even more varieties were bred for specific regions. For example, semi-dwarfs were bred that did not grow excessive foliage, reducing the amount of transpiration and so requiring less water. These could be grown in more arid zones. Secondly, break crops were used, alternate crops such as canola that did not host wheat diseases so broke the disease cycle for wheat. Breaks growing pasture were made into hay and silage to cut down on weed seed setting. For any remaining weeds very specific herbicides were used at precise amounts. Tillage was generally reduced, even to the single pass for sowing the crop. Sowing could be guided by a Global Positioning System (GPS) to sow midway between the rows of stubble, which then acted as a mulch. With so little soil disturbance there was less breakdown of organic matter and a slower release of soil nitrogen. Now soil analysis and crop growth modelling are applied to plant needs: for instance, a small amount of nitrogen fertiliser may sometimes be added at sowing, retaining the organic nitrogen till later. It is all aimed to give the highest yield at lowest possible cost and to reduce greenhouse gas emissions.

As can be seen from the graph, through manipulation of basically the same crop ecosystem, there was a yield of grain about three times that of earlier years. Understandably, the attitude of most managers is that farmers will never arrive at sustainable cropping, as they strive to ever improve yields and efficiency with new innovations and adaptable behaviour. The new behaviours can develop from ideas with a range of origins: research by agencies, ideas developed by farmers, crossovers from other industries, like the computer technologies. The Zero-Till approach, now adopted in nearly 90% of cropping in Australia and spreading round the world, was developed in the wheat belt of Western Australia largely though the persistence and 'noise' of one individual scientist, Bill Crabtree, now warmly called No-Till Bill (6).

Drought is an ever-present phenomenon, in some part or other of the wheat belt, and the levelling out of yield in Phase IV in the 2000s is indicative of a widespread drought. The control of weeds which can compete with the crop for soil moisture and plant nutrients has always been important and a quest for successful control was in earlier years responsible for many of the practices that have been maligned by conservationists, including excess tillage and chemical use. In Phase IV two practices are relevant. Don't let the weeds seed in the years before, by including hay and silage cut before seed set, and then heavy grazing with sheep. Finally, if necessary, spray with low dose herbicides with spray unit nozzles that are activated by a camera to pick up images of the weeds. This approach will reduce costs and usage of herbicides to a few millilitres per hectare.

Grouping all of these adaptations together has meant that the arid boundary of cropping land has been pushed out further in arid zones than in other parts of the world. Dr David Smith, one of the authors, has described the ecological history of the southern regions of Australia in his book, *Natural Gain in the Grazing Lands of Southern Australia* (21) and, *Greening the arid boundary* (22). The specific management of the semiarid boundary ecosystems is described. Though yields are low by European standards, the low inputs and economies of scale make for profitable production.

Green revolutions

Though rice has been extensively grown in many developing countries for centuries, in the middle decades of the 20th century Norman Borlaug, through the International Research Centres, promoted the use of short-strawed varieties and precise amounts of fertiliser, so sweeping together the best of agronomy and plant breeding. By the 1970s there was a substantial increase in crop yields and a reduction in hunger and famine. The whole movement had widespread publicity under the title of The Green Revolution. However, it was not really a revolution, but rather a bringing of knowledge and discipline to subsistence farming. So, farmers could carry out the same operations as before, but with precision and an enhanced level of skill, to give higher yields. That there have been complaints of side effects in recent years simply confirms that most change has some downsides as well as upsides and a never-ending quest for better systems is essential – not just a defined and noisy revolution.

Thus, it is no surprise that some major technologies adopted by agriculture in the last few centuries have been in contention with conservationists. One was the idea of not eating the produce fresh but to grind it up, or heat treat it, or preserve produce in salt, sugar or alcohol. For grinding, crude mortars and pestles were devised, which are still seen in various shapes and sizes in Africa today. Subsequently, after treatment, seed of a crop could be combined with other foods and food-grade materials to make new composite foods and be transported around the world. Though these operations are not the direct province of the modern farmer, they have been challenged by interest groups, in terms of use of energy resources and greenhouse gas emissions.

A perhaps more real green 'revolution' came about in Niger, in the Sahara region of Africa when large podded Australian Acacia trees were introduced in the 1980s, with many benefits (18). Being legumes, they fix atmospheric nitrogen. They are also an excellent break-wind. The foliage is a rich livestock feed for about six months of the year. The seeds are high in protein, and can be ground into a flour, which can enrich people's diets and provide some medicinal benefits. The limbs of the trees provide firewood. The introduction of this new tree into the ecosystems has changed the barren landscape and enriched people's lives.

Managing agricultural ecosystems

Changes in energy supply have had a huge effect on ecosystem management. After a long history of humans only having their own muscle power to cultivate, lift and pull, energy was provided by the beasts of burden, like the oxen, donkey and horse. At first this was in the field only, then the whim, an animal walking in a circle providing power through a shaft for grinding corn and pumping water. A little later came water power turning water wheels, then, much later engines running on fossil fuels, even mobile ones as in the tractor. It all became so much easier, especially with the wheel. Till, till, till, and cart to a better/more distant market.

One downside was that the draught animals had to be fed, so they used up feed, or at least land area, that was otherwise available for human food production. Inventing engines and using ancient stores of energy was like discovering vast new lands, and made a huge contribution to reducing famine. Then, farmers had to find money to buy the fuel, so becoming more and more dependent on fossil fuels – one of the conflicts with conservation. Nevertheless, some more recently have dreamed of growing their own fuel, even becoming sellers of bio-fuel crops.

Specialist machines were made to perform different tasks, for instance, mouldboard ploughs to turn over the surface soil and bury plant residues, discs to chop up plant residues, useful when clearing bush, tines to rip deeper into the ground and open it up for deeper root penetration, and rotary hoes to fine-chop plant residues – though they tended to beat the soil so it set hard. Rollers helped to break up clods, though sometimes compacting the soil again. The stump-jump plough was a clever innovation, greatly assisting adaptive behaviour in land clearing.

The coming of no-till mentioned above was quite an amazing reversal, occurring in the late 1990s. In terms of impact this was a full circle back to our cavewoman's digging stick. Tractor power enabled farmers to use multi-row 'digging sticks' attached to a steel frame, with a huge saving in human effort. The success of zero-till has been wonderful for most crop-land soils, despite the increased risk of damage to crops by slugs and snails. It has been made even more potent by the very precise technologies for control of weeds.

Instead of just getting the poo and pee from the cave dwellers, there was in due course recognition of the value of other materials, that we call fertilisers, containing plant nutrients. In recent decades application of plant nutrients has become a very exact science, based on soil analysis, modelling of availability of nutrients in relation to climatic factors, so minimising excess use and virtually eliminating drainage or run-off. At harvest time the machine produces a yield map for the field, enabling recognition of areas that need further study and special treatment. Bundled together and integrated into crop models the system is called Precision Farming, which is a triumph of adaptive behaviour. It brings together new plant nutrient tracing techniques such as spectroscopy, the latest IT, cameras, GPS receivers and clever machinery makers, modifying all of the things that the early farmers did. In recent years this has meant less and less impact on the environment and maximising outputs per unit of energy, water and land area.

The recognition of moisture stress in their plants would have come quite early in human history, and no doubt some water was added, rather limited by the availability of vessels to carry it. It is hard for modern people to credit the value of lightweight goat skins. In due course came the moving of earth to make channels, often hundreds of kilometres long, then dams, and in very recent times, pipes of steel, concrete and plastics have made so much possible – diameters up to four metres can carry huge volumes. This has, however, brought deep conflict with environmentalists, especially as providing more water in one place so often means having deprived another. Further, the soils of an ecosystem have been developed under a particular rainfall pattern, so that the new watering regime completely alters the hydrological balance. As a result, there are huge management challenges, such as redistribution of salt in the ecosystem.

As part of recognising ecosystems in agriculture areas there has been emphasis on the whole landscape, especially water catchments, as critical entities. This includes the impact of land use on water run-off and the place of trees in the landscape. New techniques for overall management have been promulgated through community activities like Landcare, which is now an international movement.

Overall, there is a vast knowledge of plant growth processes, and a greater range of technologies relating to actually growing plants. Collectively these provide opportunities for a variety of production systems, including urban gardens, more specialist cropping and the generation of interest in plant culture.

This can all be distilled into four clusters of activities, each with their own peculiar environmental challenges:

- Exploration, plant selection and breeding.
- Soil management and seed planting, and plant nutrient management.
- Animal and forage management.
- Vegetation management.

Our cave woman was an early plant selector. Considering her as part of the ecosystem, the various things around her, what would have been the impact of her decision to plant some seeds at a new location? At its new site the flowers of her plants might have received some slightly different pollen, and if she, or her children, kept some seeds and planted them, they might well have discerned differences. If there was an even slightly different ripening time different birds might have been attracted. For her there would have been less effort in feeding her family, with more time and energy for other things. We assume people to be thinkers, who recognised that a benefit from one new planting would surely lead to more. For example, to develop a definition of plants needed to fill gaps in the diet, and a search of a larger area for new useful material. One can imagine a search for plants that did not seem to be attacked by diseases such as rusts, even insects such as locusts.

Would it have occurred to them to give preference to local plants? How would they define local? What could limit the area? Would anyone in the 'clan' argue for staying within the valley, so using only plants that might be called 'our' plants, natives? If the cave was coastal and things like coconuts washed up on the shore would they be rejected as foreign, coming from overseas? In fact, as people moved further and further about the world there was widespread movement of plant material, sometimes deliberately, and sometimes accidentally. In the new colonies in the 1700 and 1800s there were Plant Introduction and Acclimatisation Societies, which deliberately introduced and tested new plant material.

In the relatively recent past there has been a move to insist that the present native species should be used. Some base this on a sort of loyalty, others consider that surely it is logical that native plants growing on a site are the best that could be on that site for every purpose. For instance, some people suggest plants introduced, like roses, plane trees and lawn grasses, are a blot on the landscape and should not be used (10). They argue that among the 25,000 native species of plants in Australia there should be adequate choice for all purposes. There are, however, several problems with this assertion. Firstly, we can never assume that because a plant is on a certain site that it evolved there. Plants have incredible ability to disperse over long distances, either alone or helped by humans and animals, for instance, in clothing or fur. Secondly, either before leaving their 'home' land, or after import, significant effort has been put into breeding and selection of plants for human needs, which includes advanced properties like improved nutritional value, disease resistance and beauty, which are embedded in current mainstream plants. This makes these superior in traits for economic value. Thirdly, the site of the ecosystem might have been changed, such as by adding fertiliser or drainage. As a result, in many developed countries the introduced plants have been very important in increasing food production and wealth.

It is hard to know how much long-distance migration of plants there has been over time. Plants have a huge variety of dispersal mechanisms: wings that enable blowing in the wind, flotation in running water, awns that cling to fur and wool and, once it was invented, clothing. Having seeds attractive as food for an animal or bird, yet having some resistance to digestion, is a great asset, especially if the creature involved is a wanderer so the surviving seeds are passed out some distance from the parent plant. A big plus can be the nutrients in animal faeces, giving the new seedling a good start in life.

This all suggests that the cave-woman was setting a great example! She didn't balk at using a plant from 'far' away! When were special varieties recognised? One can only wonder when these early people came to understand fertilisation/pollination, by the birds and the bees! Nowadays students are sometimes taught the importance of the work on sweet peas by the German monk Mendel, and the great advance in understanding that followed Charles Darwin's thinking on evolution. One important step for intelligent people was to recognise they could exercise some control, so to become accessories after the fact of new 'crosses', and even become involved in new plant creations. Specialists called themselves plant breeders.

One can ponder how large a range of plant material did the cave woman have in her domain? In modern times it is suggested great diversity would give more food security, that humans have imperilled food supply by narrowing to less than ten major staple food species. However, most of these staples have a large number of distinct varieties, or cultivars, as they are called when they result from plant breeding. The characteristics and tolerances of the varieties, such as disease resistance, are well known. More and more have had their genes mapped. The result is that one staple crop may have hundreds of variants grown, thus the simple number of species is a misleading guide to the huge range of plant material that can be utilised. For instance, the third most important staple crop, after wheat and rice, the potato, has 5,000 different variants grown, so that is becoming more and more popular for specific uses, and no longer just a food for primitive people (2). Potatoes have little fat, mostly starch with good supplies of vitamins and minerals. The scientific tools used to understand these crops could be efficiently used to generate new variants with specific new properties, such as drought tolerance. In the meantime collections of 'wild' plants are made and quietly studied. What is important is that the capacity to mobilise resources if necessary be maintained. Thus, to claim problems because of too few crops can be challenged – it shows poor understanding. Nevertheless, other issues remain, such as the reduced diversity of pollinating insects.

Even if left growing quietly down the valley it is likely that the bees or the wind would periodically have carried pollen from such plants so as to give new seedlings that looked different or fruit that tasted different. Later relatives of the original plant could be recognised as different enough to have a different name. Then there are mutants: a familiar one is the nectarine, which arose from peach stock.

The understanding of genes and meiosis (the fusing of genes at fertilisation) added to The Knowledge was one of the great leaps, soon leading to humans 'crossing' of plants or animals, and the creation of special purpose plants or animals. At first, plant crossing was laborious and time consuming, to grow hundreds of plants and pollinate them, to get a few new crosses. Recently, microscopic and other technologies have enabled much more certain transfer of genes from a much wider 'family'. Believers in evolution know that, if the genes fit, the different individuals are related even if very, very distantly. So-called Genetic Manipulation is not unnatural! GM cotton, incorporating bacterial DNA, has 'saved' the use of vast amounts of chemicals. Programs to produce bananas and rice with important nutritional and health attributes are promising benefit for a large number of humans. Who gains the financial rewards is another issue and must be dealt with, but to deny humanity by demonising the process shows ignorance of the continuing need for adaptations.

Understanding that the soil was such an important source of plant nutrients was a significant gain in knowledge but precision awaited some understanding of science. The Romans had some ideas on soil and plant nutrient management, valuing legumes., and a lot has been learned since – though not widely enough known in things like carbon sequestration. Notwithstanding, even today many people do not understand that nutrients are only taken up in an inorganic form in solution in soil water and thence plant sap. So, the addition of organic materials to the soil does not directly affect growth of plants. The pH of the soil affects the solubility of various nutrients, so managing pH is important.

The cave woman would have 'managed' the urine and faeces, which were quaintly called night soil once there were towns, and piss and poo in some cruder modern circles. We can imagine she put it on the new plants, with good results. It is not hard to see some trees getting much more than others, such as the ones closer to the cave. She then noticed these as growing more prolifically. Did she ponder the response to urine being just a moisture effect, or also recognise it as 'good stuff'. Probably such things would have been observed but not explained until the 'invention' of chemistry.

There is little argument that the ideal is the nearest possible to full return to the soil of the nutrients removed in the crop, with any shortfall defined and strategies devised to make up the difference. Yet in many ways the development of towns and cities has brought about less sustainable management, with the construction of sewerage systems taking all materials well outside the towns and often discharging them into the sea. But, it is unfair to blame developing agriculture for this: it was recognised that human diseases could be circulated through reuse of the human wastes on crops and this was banned in many countries. Nevertheless, safer recycling of human waste by modern treatment technologies can provide recycled water to irrigate crops and biosolids that can be used as a renewable fertiliser and soil conditioner. These technologies and associated government regulations ensure that products from recycling human waste are safer to use on farms. Also, for example, to minimise human contact, biosolids can be injected under the soil, close to the roots of plants, especially of tree crops. Biosolids, along with other organic fertilisers, can provide plant nutrients like phosphorus and potash.

There is a paradox in the history of intensive animal management. Keeping hens in cages made it very easy to capture the chicken manure and sell it for use on vegetable crops and mushroom composting floors, and even to apply it on farmland as part of organic farming. It is nigh impossible to collect the manure from free-range operations and the alternative materials for organic are variable and lower in value. Other material is often expensive through transport costs. Some have attempted to run hens integrated with animal grazing, but over much of the world there is the problem of predators such as foxes.

Managing plant nutrients

It cannot be stated too many times, that after the spark of life itself, the growth of the green plant is arguably the next greatest miracle on earth. It absorbs CO_2 gas from the atmosphere, captures external energy from the sun, stores it through photosynthesis, then releases the energy when needed, and returns the carbon as new CO_2. Phosphorus is an absolutely vital element here as a component of chlorophyll, the green pigment. In the process free oxygen is released, thus making other life possible on the planet. In line with this Genesis states, "... and as I give

96

you the green plants, I give you everything." (4), which is a remarkable early wording! It should never be forgotten that this photosynthesis is part of a cycle that is vital to agriculture. The cave folk would surely have taken greenness of plants for granted. They would have realised that there was better growth under the sunny season, but putting it into chemical and energy equations is very recent. It is all so very pertinent to understanding the relationship of agricultural activities to conservation issues and especially climate change.

It is hard to imagine not having that knowledge but the debates about carbon cycles suggest that many people have a lot more learning to do. Some people think that sequestration is a matter of digging a hole, putting in some carbon and filling in the hole. Rather it means stimulating these biological cycles, especially for carbon and nitrogen, ensuring there is enough phosphate and sulphur present. As a result, plants and soil organisms will build more of the compounds that contain carbon, nitrogen, sulphur and phosphorus. Cycles for nitrogen and phosphorus are shown in Figures 5.2 and 5.3, respectively. All must recognise that while farming produces food it is also a giant carbon sequestration system!

The cave woman took her digging stick and 'cultivated' the soil to make a sort of furrow, in which to plant the new seeds. The interaction with the soil of different tools led to selecting a particular type of tool. As has been described, the cultivating tool has change over time, from much the same simple shape as her stick, to a tine with wide 'feet', or a small disc, now full circle in what we now call zero-till, which mostly uses a tine about the size we imagine her stick to have been. The modern equipment has a number of these tines mounted in a row on

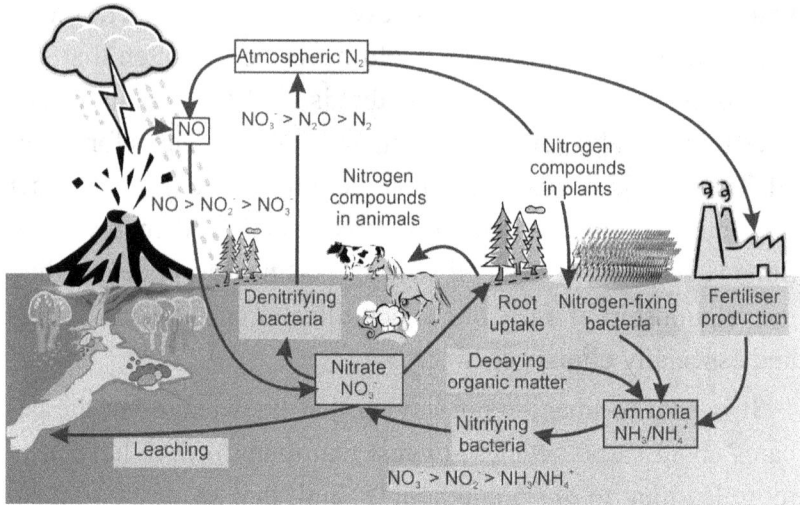

Figure 5.2 The nitrogen cycle in farming ecosystems. Cycling of nitrogenous compounds takes place in both the atmosphere, top white area, and soil, bottom grey area. Nitrogenous compounds shown are: N_2, nitrogen gas; NO_3^-, nitrate; NO_2^-, nitrite; NO, nitric oxide; N_2O, nitrous oxide; NH_3/NH_4^+, ammonia. Nitrate is the key nitrogen compound required for growth of crops. To maintain growth of crops and pastures nitrate is added to land by nitrogen-fixing bacteria that live in the soil or by fertilisers that contain nitrogen in the form of ammonia.

a frame, all pulled forward together by a tractor. The whole unit is generally guided by a satellite through GPS receivers in such a way that this year's crop is midway between last year's rows and the residue of the last year's crop used as a soil mulch.

The amount of tillage of early farming was probably limited by the availability of energetic humans with hoes or, later, the presence of draught animals. Much of the tillage in Africa is still done by 'digging sticks', a wooden tool, sometimes with a steel tip, mounted as a sort of plough, pulled through the soil by a mule or some other animal. The plough must be light enough to be carried over the shoulder of the farmer as he walks behind his mule to one of the fields of his farm. The farm is likely fragmented through inheritance, made up of several strips of land, not always next to another. In yet other places all tillage is done by women wielding heavy, blunt, cast iron hoes. Though light, wide pressed-steel hoes would be a great move forward, one

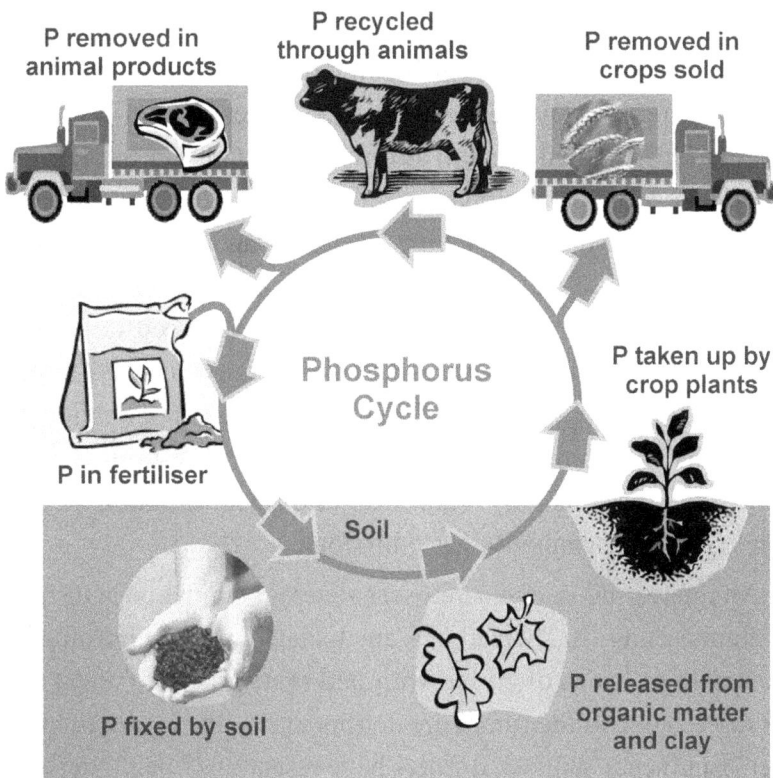

Figure 5.3 The phosphorus (P) cycle in farming ecosystems. To maintain growths of crops and pastures farmers utilise land fertilisers that contain phosphorus (usually in the form of phosphate) to replace the phosphorus that is taken out in animal and crop products.

wonders whether tillage can be largely eliminated there too, as it has been in Australia.

So why was tillage invented? Presumably, in broad terms, to prepare the soil for the crop to grow, including the control of weeds. Modern humans know that part of this was the release of nutrients by breaking down organic matter, by aeration, into inorganic forms ready to be taken up by the plant, as well as for weed control. In the absence of cutting implements or the confining of grazing animals it was difficult to eliminate seed setting by the weeds the year before cropping. So, in preparing the field to grow a winter crop, came summer rains and weeds, and the farmer tilled the soil several times. Only in the last 50 years has there been emphasis on the knowledge of weed ecology, so minimising seed setting by weeds and maximising the value of mulch in reducing weed seed germination. Thus, before chemical herbicides were invented, tillage was used to rid the proposed crop site of plants, often dense growths, that might compete with the crop, so-called weeds. Precise application of chemicals can complete near perfect control. The preservation of organic matter is very significant in the sequestration of carbon to reduce greenhouse gas emissions.

An interesting issue that crosses several boundaries is the use of animal dung. In African peasant societies the fire burning in the centre of hut is often fed with odd materials, like wood not yet dried out, and the fumes are detrimental to the health of children. Engineers Without Borders have researched the matter and found well-dried animal dung to be superior (14) with giraffe faeces best of all. However, unless care is taken to return of the ashes evenly over the entire fields this risks adding another 'loss' arrow in our cycles of nutrients.

Animal management

Even if difficult to acquire, at quite an early stage animal meat was valued as part of the human diet. Quite recently flesh was recognised as protein, balancing the plant material, which was mostly carbohydrates. No doubt the people learned more and more about animal behaviour, making it easier to get a kill. The Aboriginals in Australia, in surely one of the most remarkable feats, invented better hunting equipment, including the truly amazing wooden boomerang, which would return to the hunter after striking the prey. Finally, Europeans brought the gun with bullets and shot. Domestication and keeping animals like sheep, and to a lesser extent goats, near the camp was a great help.

The system was often 'minding' animals, with a man, called a shepherd, in attendance limiting the movement of the animals during the day, keeping them together usually on any pasturage available, and frightening away any hungry predators, like lions. Towards nightfall the shepherd would then herd the animals into the fold – yard – for the night. A typical fold was a circle of stones, pickets or prickly bushes. These materials were piled/arranged so as to be difficult for animals to climb over. Gathering and construction must have taken a lot of work, and, unfortunately, good grazing land often has few suitable stones: it was not often the two came together as in Sardinia, where in the Bronze Age, BC, many stone shelters called 'nuraghes' were erected, with attached 'yards' to hold animals. There were hundreds of these structures.

At many places in Africa, for example, in Zimbabwe, woven thorn bush circles have long been used to confine special animals. To 'hand' feed them some bushes would have been pulled up, then in very recent times cutting hand tools such as slashers and sickles have been available. Others used dense hedge rows and stone walls to confine animals. Recently, came modern wire in various forms – plain, barbed, mesh. As described above there are many associated technologies. One just being tested is electronic beam fence lines, with a receptor on the animal turning it back near the line. Some can be used to provide many small paddocks, grazed to measured residues of green leaf to continue photosynthesis and provide 'manufacturing floor space' for carbohydrates. According to their structure and growth patterns, different pasture plants produce best under different field lay outs – it is simply not true that all are best intensively grazed at all times. It is not hard to see the importance of ecological studies of forage species. Lucerne is best grazed by large groups in many small paddocks: for phalaris and sub clover paddock size has much less importance.

Improvements over time included haymaking, in which forage material grown in a time of plenty was sun-dried, stacked, or silage, moist green fodder stored in pits. These stores were fed to animals in the season when there was insufficient growth. In recent times the processes of making both have been highly mechanised, the silage even 'packed', wrapped in plastic covered units. The finely tuned and profitable Icelandic system has been described above (see Beginnings of agriculture). Not only have we seen huge improvements in the ability to contain animals, both for convenience and care for the grazed plants, but also in access to water that is now able to be distributed widely using cheap plastic piping, and solar or wind powered pumps. This is useful for intensive rotational grazing, and also for very extensive rangeland grazing. With all this goes responsibility for good conservation management of the forage and care of the soil cover.

Some people claim ownership of the words 'holistic grazing' as describing their system as superior. One such is Allan Savory in Africa, promoted in Australia by the Soils for Life movement (19). It is based on fear of circling lions ensuring the wilde-bestes (gnus) in large groups have completely grazed out their patch of pasture, for generally no more than three days, before they desperately break out and seek new pasture. The original area is then allowed to recover, over some months, even nine. Savory considers this similar in function to having many small paddocks. Research has been carried out in Europe and Austra-lia for generations with debates about small paddocks v. bigger paddocks, rotational grazing/on-off grazing v. set stocking, etc. Dairy farmers on dryland as well as irrigation farms have long practiced a form of small field/large herd grazing, usually us-ing electric fencing. Small paddocks mean more fences, more water points and often more labour. Gross margins are generally higher under some circumstances, but show little gain under oth-ers, and pasture quality is a factor. Some of Savory's disciples make the remarkable claim that with a system of small paddocks 'in a single blow the battle against weeds is won'. Few farming people would believe him. Prickly thistles? Bathurst burrs with nasty thorns? They also cite seven-fold increases in productiv-ity. Comparisons are very difficult, with so many variables. For example, can people who adopt intensive grazing by using small paddocks are likely to at the same time improve the species composition and use precise inputs of fertiliser? Otherwise, the transition from grazing shrubby native vegetation to a well fer-tilised pasture of selected pasture plants and quite large fenced paddocks can provide many multiple increases in productivity – even twenty-fold.

Forage management, which involves sowing additional species, improving growth of some plants, keeping animals off certain areas and depending on modern technologies, is mostly a feature of the last century or so. Strategic grazing has always been one of the 'tools' assisting in weed control, sometimes with changed patterns, sometimes with different animals. Earlier in history pasture was the volunteer growth of plants on land not needed for crops, or on common lands around towns. In the context of this study, the Aboriginal practice of 'renewing' the grasslands through burning was a brilliant early example of management.

Once animals could be confined, especially if there was private land holding, farmers gained an interest in management of what grew in fields. A great example in Europe was work in the early 1900s at the Welsh plant Breeding Station at Aberystwyth, Wales, UK. That fortuitously connected to work at the Waite Institute in Southern Australia and passed on knowledge, deeply influencing Australian thinking. The early focus was on selecting species, including, especially, perennial grasses such as rye grass and cocksfoot and phalaris. Then came understanding of plant nutrition and, especially in southern Australia, perceptions of the potential of large areas of soil low in plant nutrients. Defining the need for trace/minor elements for plants brought millions of hectares of sandy soils in southern Western Australia into production in the three decades from 1950. Similar successes occurred in the south-east of South Australia and western Victoria. This usually involved complete replacement of the native vegetation, which had been adapted to the deficient soil, and sowing introduced species, with emphasis on legumes that raise the nitrogen and organic matter level of soils. In their native state these areas had near zero carrying capacity, even for kangaroos. Under the new system carrying capacity was easily 10-12 dry sheep per hectare (less if pregnant or lactating ewes).

This was effectively a total re-make of the ecosystems, one of the most controversial aspects of agriculture, which at times caused savage conflict with conservation interests. Yet there is plenty of evidence that over the ages, during the evolution of plants, few places were an 'island'. The flora of any place at any time was to a large extent an accident of history, the result of evolution from some plants present at the formation of the land mass or when isolating barriers like deserts developed. Each land mass has its own history, some old in form, some new, such as in deposit of soil by floods or lava flows from volcanos. Sometimes there would have been continual arrival of new plants to the site from nearby lands, carried by birds or animals. Where there was a long distance across the sea to the nearest land, as in the case of Australia, there would have been little new material arriving and little going elsewhere. Thus, the claim that it was the best that could be, beginning with the limited material present, was true. But it was not the best that could ever be. What is 'best' is a challenge and usually relates to yields of leaves, seeds, having great flowers, or producing useful timber.

Once boats carried livestock from Europe, for instance from UK, to Australia, in the 19th century, some ships called into Mediterranean ports to get fodder, inevitably including seeds of local plants, natives to the Mediterranean area, which was described as having a Mediterranean climate – a distinctly wet cool winter season and a hot dry summer. When the ships were cleaned at Australian ports there was no quarantine, so cleanings were dumped near the ports. When seeds germinated there was a sorting out of those new species suitable for the climate, which happened to be similar to that of the pick-up ports. It was home from home! One of the most important arrivals was *Trifolium subterraneum* (subterranean – sub, for short) – clover, which had evolved on the limited area of acid soils near the Mediterranean Sea and was a small plant, a minor roadside 'weed' in several countries, not much contributing to animal forage ecosystems. It probably landed from ships at several places, one important one being Albany in Western Australia, in cleanings from sheep's pens. It was suited to the vast areas of acid soils across southern Australia, surviving but not prospering as the soils were mostly deficient in phosphorus and some other important nutrients. A few decades later, about 1880, the idea of using manufactured fertilisers (especially phosphate, called super) on wheat crops arrived in Australia. Thus, after cropping some fields had raised levels of phosphate and if clover was present it responded dramatically producing vastly more fodder, four to ten times, so was able to feed a lot of sheep and cattle. The kangaroos loved it, grazing with the sheep.

In due course the puzzle as to why clover was so much more luxuriant than in Europe was successfully worked out: the plant had a cold requirement to initiate flowering. Thus, the new clover plants grew leaves until they had accumulated the effect of enough cold nights for the plant growing point to cease producing leaves and to begin producing flowers. In Europe the winds from the Arctic over land are dry and cold, whereas the southerlies of Australia, coming over the Southern Ocean, are cool and moist. So, in southern Australia it takes longer for the plants to accumulate the cold, and in that time they grow more leaves, that is a lot more forage for animals than in Europe. Further, being a legume, using bacteria on its roots to fix nitrogen from the atmosphere, it fixed a lot of nitrogen, enabling the build-up of organic matter, transforming soils. It vastly increased the productivity of the poor soils in southern Australia. Remarkably, there were variants of the clover. Some of these took longer to set seed, that is, suited localities with more and longer rainfall. In California and Chile it accumulated the effect of cold temperatures more quickly, so that it grew less forage and fixed less nitrogen.

Sub clover had another feature which proved of great value in Australia. The seed is in a spiny burr/pod, which the plant buries in the surface layers of the soils – the scientific term is negative geotrophy. Sheep lie down a lot and pick up the burrs in their wool, dropping them in a new place, a neat way of spreading. However, the seed could not be easily 'cleaned', that is broken out of the burr and separated from the other debris, a very real problem for sales. It took another migrant entity to fix this: Ronald Kaesler a German blacksmith in the town of Hahndorf in South Australia, who built an effective seed /cleaner/thresher. The quantity of seed harvested and sold rose rapidly and the plant was widely sown, bringing prosperity to the region. This is a reminder of the complex nature of progress, which at times includes great benefits from human migrants with their particular skills.

Old plants in new homes

In what came to be one of the great ecosystem changes in human history, sub clover was widely sown in the 1900s. Because there are a number of varieties, adaptation in the face of global warming should not be too difficult. This classic case puts down forever any assertion that plants evolved elsewhere are not adaptable to Australian conditions. Clover was even better adapted. Over the last 60 years the contribution of clover plus phosphate to the Australian economy has been huge (the value of the nitrogen fixed has been calculated as $5 to $10 billion per annum) – and will continue.

There are many examples on every continent, such as the cereal crops wheat, oats and barley that originated in Central Asia and spread to all occupied continents. All these cases are also hugely important in the study of plant ecology. Again, looking at Australia, there are no locally occurring plants that in any way approach such a level of usefulness. However, there is one quite surprising connection: oats which is considered to have originated in Asia Minor is a relatively close 'cousin' of Wallaby grass, a Danthonia species, one of the widespread (so-called) native grasses of Australia. It would seem most likely that seeds of an ancient ancestor of oats were somehow carried to new sites and to the earlier great southern land mass, and finally evolved into the Danthonia of today's Australia. Thus, one can ask the purists who define a native as 'a plant that evolved here' Are you quite sure that Danthonia is a native – how much evolution occurred on the way?

The urge to leave/keep any plant ecosystem the same, either in form or composition of species, or both, assumes that it would be so in the absence of humans – is 'natural'. Related to this is the idea that we should use land for the same vegetation types as nature had there, to mimic nature. Grassland should remain grassland, even with different species, and forest should remain forest. This fails to recognise history. Vegetation evolves on new deposits, like lava, river depositions and wind-deposited sands. What exists on a site at any one time in history is a product of what species were present, and what has been introduced, but proves nothing about the best. Then there are plants that have arrived and are at home, without becoming too much trouble, such as capeweed which apparently hitch-hiked from South Africa. This is the yellow flowered plant of the daisy family with petals, used to test if 'She loves me – She loves me not'!

What of those that become serious weeds, costing much to prevent from reducing crop yields or poisoning livestock? A weed, by definition, is any plant that is not wanted in that situation. Research to acquire The Knowledge of the physiology and anatomy and hence the ecology of a plant, especially unloved ones, is an important step in managing the ecosystems in which they occur. Quite often this can lead to reduced use of weedicides, thus the use of what is called Integrated Pest Management (IPM). Knowledge incorporated into field management practice is the first priority, with chemicals as a fall back, a last resort – but applied with precision and with consideration of both cost and ecological damage.

Clearly advocating no use of any introduced species in the case of Australia, which would mean no grains or fruit trees or common vegetables, is generally untenable. Australia would be battling to feed a million people, yet now it feeds its own population of more than 20 million and exports enough food for tens of millions more. What is emerging in modern times is a need to maximise returns, sometimes from human effort (Central Africa), per unit of land area (Europe), per mm of rainfall (southern Australia), and overall, increasingly, everywhere, per unit of CO_2 emitted. In Australia precision farming, as touched on above, has emerged as the powerful modern 'tool' for all of the above.

Knowing

At many points there are paradoxes: rarely do operations have all upside and no downside. Abandoning the many passes with tillage machinery to control weeds, so improving soil structure and raising soil organic matter and increasing carbon sequestration, has come, through generally precisely applying chemical herbicides. Use of these chemicals, without understanding the context, has brought severe criticism from groups, especially the organic food movement and the Soils for Life group. As critics, both of these groups do not seem to understand the latter-day farming motto 'We must know', to analyse aiming at maximum yield and minimum unwanted impact, though rarely zero, in any system. Know is now said to be the most important four letter word on the farm, supplanting some others.

It is essential that the composition of all inputs be known, fitting into input/output models. A good example is the composition of organic material added in organic farming, which is often not really known and hence yields are typically lower, compared to yields from mainstream commercial farming. These yield differences depend on system and site characteristics, and range from 5% lower organic yields (rain-fed legumes and perennials on weak-acidic to weak-alkaline soils), 13% lower yield when best organic practices are used), to 34% lower yields (when the mainstream and organic systems are most comparable (20). Also, for organic farming freight and labour costs are typically higher per tonne of product than for mainstream farming, due to the differences in scale. When the land area needed to produce organic additives is included, about 50% more land is needed to produce the same amount of food. Concurrently, emissions of CO_2 per tonne of food produced works against the targets for reducing GHG emissions. Thus, its use is questionable unless the food value is much higher than the product from mainstream commercial farms, and in most independent studies it is not. To date there is no proven evidence suggesting significant nutritional differences between organic and mainstream produced food (8, 24) so the advocacy of organic systems is questionable. Fortunately, despite a lot of promotion, organic farming remains a small percentage, possibly less than 1% of the world's crop area. It has been estimated that, if adopted as the main system, agriculture would struggle to feed just 4 billion people (5).

This lack of precision and knowing also applies to the making and use of biochar. There is no defined composition and it is often sold without analysis on a label. Its method of manufacture is defined as burning residues under anaerobic conditions, leaving between 30% and 80% elemental carbon (C). But what is 'the other stuff '? This varies according to the source of the waste. For example, two 'Biochars' were described recently (12). One product from poultry litter had total phosphorus (P) 3.4% and total nitrogen (N) 0.8%, while the other from green plant waste had 0.01% P and 0.14% N. The first would boost crop yields, while the second would be virtually useless as a source of plant nutrients, though could still be useful as a soil conditioner or for carbon storage. Imagine doing fertilizer use planning if one's supplies had no definition and varied widely, as in this example.

The wood and the trees

The discussion of agricultural ecosystems frequently includes trees – though they might at times seem a separate domain, as forestry, there is no clear line. Through early human history firewood was a vital part of life, then gradually a construction material. In modern times trees are an integral part of the farming landscape and ecosystems and managing them is as important as managing the pastures and crops. Conflict about their use and/or removal is a major element in the conservation and environment debate. Sweeping statements are sometimes made about the area of 'forest' removed by land clearing, even though, for instance in southern Australia, these were often stunted trees. There are various definitions. In the subject discipline of Botany, a forest is a place where the trunk of the trees (the bole) is longer than the tops, the foliage. The Government of South Australia defines a forest as an area where trees grow more than two metres tall and shade more than 20% of the ground. (7). Yet, some environmental activists know no such definition and in their eyes any large plants grouped together, of whatever shape or height, are deemed to form a forest. In many cases a dense, actively growing pasture is far superior to sparse scrub in balancing carbon.

Shelter from the elements and even marauding animals was obviously important early in human history. Our cave woman and her family lived in a cave, a ready-made shelter. What else was there? What about timber, from trees? Before there were appropriate tools, timber was hard to use. Windfalls of limbs would have been coveted as firewood. Imagine cutting down a tree with a stone axe, or even in quite recent times, say 3,000 years ago, with rather crude metal axes! Breaking off branches or palm fronds might have provided short-lived shelter.

Though early humans would have posed little threat to trees, just in the last few hundred years came toothed saws to fell trees and, to cut slabs, mills operated by whims, with a horse or donkey walking in a circle to drive a saw bench, an ingenious contraption, or a saw driven by water power. Very recently with engine or electric powered mills timber can be used to make any shaped building so there is a very different attitude to trees and timber. Structures to confine animals have been constructed from trees: fences were, until about 200 years ago, post and rail. Then wire was invented in the 1800s, and combined with fewer posts, this has greatly eased the pressure on tree cover.

In the early period of European settlement in Australia timber was the material for all structures, including homes, barns, bridges, fencing, ships, and in mining for pit props and boilers. It is suggested that farming often followed into areas where there had been wood harvesting for other purposes, such as pit props and smelters in mining (3). It has been suggested that a million tonnes of timber was cut in the peak year of Bendigo mines – for instance mine-shaft props and firing boilers. Agriculture followed.

Australia is said to have given the world a great gift in the Eucalypt tree. It only occurred naturally in Australia and New Guinea, evolving into a huge range of species, more than 500, varying from majestic forest trees that are more than 60 metres tall, to handsome spreading trees located in grassland landscapes, to shrubby members a couple of metres tall. It has been widely planted and thrived all over the world and has been a boon. For instance, it fuelled railway expansion in Brazil, and in central Africa native people have developed great skill in handcutting thin slabs. The eucalypts provide good honey, and slabs, among many uses, are made into beehives, so greatly increasing honey yield without destructive harvesting. Some people make controversial claims about Eucalypts excessive water use, but, logically, any tree that grows big and gives shade must use water.

Early humans, such as the cavewoman, would have kept a fire burning, at times for warmth, at times for cooking food, and at times for deterring animals such as lions and wolves. Whatever, the women put a huge amount of effort into collecting enough dry wood to keep a fire going, and efforts were only lessened in much later times when reasonably good axes were available, and latterly, toothed saws. The diaries of one Australian farm family for the 1930s record that, even with an axe and hand saw, it took roughly one third of the father's time to provide wood for the family fires.

In Africa, even today, much time goes into collecting fire-wood and keeping a fire burning in the centre of the round hut. A project has been tested in Senegal where the huts were made slightly elliptical, not quite round. The fire was put at one 'end', not in the centre, and to ensure smoke escaped, a single chimney pot was put on the top of the roof. Further, the fire was contained by a small wall with an aperture to push the wood through. Cooking vessels could be set on this wall instead of being pre-cariously balanced on the fire. The new arrangement reduced spillage of food by at least 70%, injuries to children through contact with the fire by 90% and, because the wood pieces could be pushed into the fire only when needed, wood consumption was halved. Overall it had a dramatic effect on women's lives: less waste of food, less fixing children's burns, less than half the time collecting firewood. It is the walking/carrying as well as the collecting that consumes time and energy. Ecologically, there was a reduced impact of firewood collection on the woodland. In fact, attention could be given to planting a small plantation near the village, which in four or five years could generate enough wood to make the system sustainable. The women would have such a large saving of time that they could give much better care to their families.

The removal of tree and shrub vegetation to provide grazing or clear spaces for planting food crops would have been a gradual development, even with rotation as in the slash and burn described previously, also the burning of grass near waterholes by the Aboriginals in Australia. The removal of tree and shrub vegetation over large areas and sowing of introduced crop and pasture species has been an important part of the economic development of Australia.

Managing forest ecosystems in developed countries has become a field of conflict between preservers of native forests and users of timber products with powerful forces advocating leaving native forests alone and using plantations for all timber and paper. It is not widely recognised that forests go through a sort of internal cycling, albeit over long periods, even as long as 100 years. It is often a later part of the cycle when debris has accumulated that carries a hot forest fire and there is contention where people are allowed to live in forested areas that carry hot wild fires. The burning releases nutrients and often breaks dormancy in seeds, so restarting the cycle of plant life. Certain old growth forest areas must be protected absolutely, better than 'left to nature', by being actively protected, but there are large areas of native forest that could be managed for a variety of outcomes, in mosaics of clear felling and selections, or with rotations from 50 to 100 years. The various stages can provide for the full range of community needs, plenty of forest 'products' for all. Examples of needs are a fine habitat for wildlife, recreation for humans and a timber harvesting stage. In Victoria, Australia, the Greens political party policy is that all timber production must come from special plantations, which means that vast areas of good agricultural country will have to be planted to produce timber, further stressing the food base of the planet.

Further conflict arises because it is not often enough recognised that there are areas of land either too recent in soil formation for trees to have arrived – like the basalt plains – or they have recently arrived but the newly forming soil is of very low fertility. In many cases the arrival of humans who bring trees and plant them for livestock shelter and firewood has meant there are now far more trees present in the landscape, or larger and better trees, even if they tend to be in lines along fences or along roadways. In southern Australia there are millions of hectares of quite recent coastal sand-plains where the landscape had been transformed into very productive land with many new trees in the landscape.

It is sometimes alleged that scientists are so impressed with photosynthesis that they see no alternative to the green plant as a basis for feeding the people of the planet. There are of course the creatures of the sea, but even here at the bottom of the food chain there are green plants, like seaweed and phytoplankton. The study of marine ecosystems, and even commercial sea creature farming is in its infancy. But what is the scope for innovative thinking about alternative systems? Berhan Ahmed (1), an Eritrean who migrated to Australia and has become an expert on termites, suggests we should consider all possibilities, for instance, the utilisation of debris after forest trees have been harvested. Leaves might be fed to specially bred meat producing lines of domesticated koalas, an Australian native animal under threat of extinction. Woody waste might be wind-rowed and 'seeded' with termites, to be fed to poultry in barns or young fish in ponds. Methane from the termites may also be captured and used to run a small electricity station. Who can predict what imagination and new technologies will conjure? All users of ecosystems must understand each other as society faces new prospects.

Future Makers

The people must be fed! The people growing food commercially must get an adequate return. The workers in the industry must be fairly treated. And the productivity of the ecosystems must go on and on.

In the past a raft of new technologies have been involved, again, some having only a slight impact on the environment, some massive. Some have been based on limited knowledge – a tendency to suck it and see! All have upsides and downsides, the latter sometimes evident after long use. A good example is pasture legumes, which so prolifically fix nitrogen that there is acidification of the soil, requiring liming. This all underlines the need for explicit analysis of processes and research into problems. A useful definition of sustainable agriculture is farming to which society is committing enough resources to identify the problems, research answers to them and have amelioration adopted to minimise things like environmental impact.

All interested players must have an open and transparent approach to main stream, mostly commercial, farming and accept it as essential to human beings on the planet. All involved in ecosystem management – even if only to be critics – must have an understanding of the basic processes, reading books such as, *Rain and Shine* (23). Evidence-based information must be respected. Advocates of alternative agriculture all too often make statements that demonise mainstream agriculture with unfounded general statements and without subjecting their own activity to scrutiny. Organic systems do not provide nutrient balance sheets: their inputs of organic fertiliser/material are not usually analysed and may not have enough of the key nutrients like phosphorus to replace that removed by the crop. Or, they may have nutrients like nitrogen in excess of needs, risking leaching and run-off. The energy used to provide and transport these nutrients in bulky material, also embedded in various processes, may not be counted. Thus, it is not enough to assert the name of the system with inference about inputs and outputs: there must be analysis. Organic food production is hugely variable in yield, generally lower per unit of land and production per unit of fossil fuel, so to feed a given number of people its contributing to higher carbon dioxide levels is higher. It is also largely oblivious to major challenges, like managing the earth's phosphate, labelling organic as a cure-all.

Maintaining diversity is often seen as a given as long as agriculture can be kept out of the area. Often, however, the total variety is increased if it is introduced and native species are also counted. Further, a systematic approach, associated with rapidly identifying DNA, will play a great part in the achievements of the biological sciences. This will also help define the biodiversity we are trying to protect.

All players must seek to understand other systems and where they 'fit' globally. For instance, some complex units with a mix of enterprise on a small scale, like the Polyface Farm, have a place, particularly in the lifestyle of small scale and part-time farmers, and their produce may be traded at local markets. Though only capable of supporting a small proportion of the food supply to the world, there are other values quantified differently from on a mainstream farm. Prices may be higher under the guise of being special, readily paid by that stratum of society.

The important issue is that this operation should not be at the expense of demonising their commercial counterparts and society must be under no illusion about the widespread applicability of close localisation.

Finally, it is interesting to ponder ecosystems managed with limited understanding and what could be achieved for some currently deprived groups of humans. The internationalism of science is very important. There is a need for good-hearted missionaries and Non-Government Organisations to be accompanied by science and be informed on good practice. There have been, and continue to be, interesting challenges. In places like Europe and Australia a key objective in managing swards of pasture was to maximise growth and animal production, and, in recent years, maximum sequestration of carbon sometimes takes precedence.

New research will enlighten – and sometimes challenge – traditional practices. One example is grazing management. In Australia, grazing practice has long been based on early research showing that grazing to leave a certain amount of leaf (that is, photosynthetic) area and ensured rapid recovery, with increased overall production. This was further enhanced by sowing better adapted species and ensuring, by test plots, that adequate plant nutrients were available. This suggests that it is likely that production from the Serengeti would be increased if areas were fenced and predators managed, existing pastures species improved by breeding and/or selection and new plants introduced from elsewhere, especially legumes to make nitrogen abundant. Possibly some closing up/resting of some areas and fodder conservation, would be valuable. Professionally managing a farming system, rather than mainly a somewhat romantic tourist curiosity, may mean livestock production could be increased substantially with meat export. Gains in productivity from the 'natural' to a managed state informed by science may mean that the people of some parts of Africa might not need aid. An added benefit is that no domesticated animal will go extinct.

It is interesting to ponder what would be the state of the Australian economy if there had not been any ecosystem change by the European settlers over the last 200 years, no introduction of species from elsewhere, no soil improvement by adding fertilisers and kangaroos had remained the grazing animal, working out their own patterns of grazing. It is likely that there would be a small fraction of the current population, living in poor circumstances, perhaps becoming grateful recipients of aid from a First World East Africa!

Conclusion

There are many activities of humans in ecosystems that would come under the heading of agriculture, from the cave woman's effort with trees, to Icelandic people overcoming the deep cold of winter, to African people growing crops with old-fashioned hoes, to Australian farmers using tractor mounted tools and satellite guidance, and so on. All, in their way, are concerned with food supply and nutrition for themselves, or others in cities. Some are mainly obsessed with the survival of their group, while many others are future makers, looking ahead to having to feed more and more people, or, increasingly, making sure the earth's resources are not consumed or exhausted, but will be sustained, even increased. They are all Future Makers.

They are also all managers of ecosystems, which are systems where a variety of living things and their processes interact. The farm managers minimise some interactions like insects eating their crop and accentuate others, like plants fixing atmospheric nitrogen. In many cases they have been involved with extremely complex interactions, often not fully understanding them until the coming of scientific support for their efforts. Most of the things they do have a downside as well as a major benefit and have continued because they have no improved alternative. Nevertheless, they have at times failed to recognise adverse impacts and so not acted to reduce them. They are at times criticised by people who fail to understand the nature of agricultural effort and the importance of some activities. It is useful to agree that agriculture comprises natural ecosystems that have been altered by the adaptive behaviour of humans, that the understandings of science and evidence based research can illuminate natural systems of life and growth and there is no excuse for not embodying this knowledge into management. Precision farming is progress in the right direction.

From the examples cited it is evident that agriculture can be described as human attempts to modify or even establish new ecosystems to serve certain specific needs of humanity. Sometimes the adaptation simply involves stimulating higher production, for example, by adding fertiliser or changing grazing arrangements, in existing ecosystems. Sometimes it involves introducing new species to the existing vegetation; in extreme cases it involves complete replacement. Sometimes it involves different arrangements for grazing animals, such as for the time of lambing.

Another group of humans have predominantly conservation aims, basically drawing on parts of the same knowledge base, using many of the same tools. Conservation is also part of modern farming. Farmers conserve soil, plantation trees and local areas of native vegetation. The challenge now is how this part of agricultural business will co-exist with new innovative food production to feed the growing world population. While many farmers eagerly innovate, these others see more virtue in things remaining the same. It is important that we all understand each other.

References

1. Ahmed, B. (2014) Personal communication.

2. Bayer CropScience AG (2013) Potato: The Global Tuber. Farming's Future, *Bayer CropScience*, Company Magazine, 1/2013: 6-9.

3. Blainey, G. (1984) *Our side of the country: The story of Victoria.* Methuen Haynes, Australia.

4. Bible quotes were taken from the Revised Standard Version: biblical parable, Mark 4: 3-9; Genesis 9:3.

5. Connor, D.J., and Mínguez, M.I. (2012) Evolution not revolution of farming systems will best feed and green the world. *Global Food Security*, 1(2): 106-113.

6. Crabtree, B. (2010) Search for Sustainability in Dryland Agriculture. Self-published.

7. Department of Primary Industries and Regions (2008) What is a forest? Government of South Australia. http://www.pir.sa.gov.au, accessed 1-10-14.

8. European Food Information Council (EUFIC) (2013) Organic food and farming: scientific facts and consumer perceptions. http://www.eufic.org, accessed 10-10-14.

9. Flannery, T. (2002) The day, the land, the people. http://www.onlineopinion.com.au, accessed 14-10-14.

10. Flannery, T. (2008). Now or Never: A Sustainable Future for Australia? *Quarterly Essay*, 31 September 2008.

11. Goldsmith, E., R. Allen, M. Allaby, J. Davoll and S. Lawrence (1972) A Blueprint for survival. *The Ecologist* 2(1): 1-22, and Penguin Books. http://www.theecologist.org/back_archive/19701999/, accessed 9-1-17.

12. Grasslands Society of Southern Australia (2010) *Newsletter*, Jan 2010.

13. Hymn: We plough the fields, and scatter. Hymn written in German by Matthias Claudius (1782); translated into English by Jane M. Campbell.

14. O'Shea (2014) Personal communication.

15. Pascose, B. (2016) Reaping Seeds of Discontent. 3010. Sept 2016, *Melbourne University Magazine*, The University of Melbourne.

16. Pollan, M. (23 April 2004) A Flood of U.S. Corn Rips at Mexico. *The Los Angeles Times*, USA.

17. Pollan, M. (2006) *The Omnivore's Dilemma: A Natural History of Four Meals*. Penguin Group (USA) Incorporated.

18. Rinaudo, A., P. Patel and L. Thomson (2002) Potential of Australian Acacias in combating hunger in semi-arid lands. *Conservation Science*, 4, 161-169. The introduction of Acacia trees into barren landscapes was largely the work of Tony Rinaudo, an Australian agricultural missionary, in the 1980s.

19. Savory A. (2013) Response to request for information on the "science" and "methodology" underpinning Holistic Management and holistic planned grazing (Updated 6-3-2013). http://www. savoryinstitute.com, accessed 30-9-14.

20. Seufert, V., N. Ramankutty and J.A. Foley (2012) Comparing the yields of organic and conventional agriculture. *Nature* (10 May 2012) 485, 229-232.

21. Smith, D.F. (2000) *Natural Gain: In the Grazing Lands of Southern Australia*. University of New South Wales Press.

22. Smith, D. F. (2011) The Greening of the Arid Boundary. *Quadrant*, 55(7-8): 94-103.

23. Smith, D.F. (2012) Rain and Shine, a simple guide to how plants grow. Connor Court Publishing, Brisbane, Australia.

24. Stanford University School of Medicine (2012) Are Organic Foods Safer or Healthier than Conventional Alternatives? A systematic review. *Annals of Internal Medicine*, 157(5), 348-366.

25. Whipple, T. (2013) Neanderthals showed signs of being cave proud. *The Times*, U.K., 4 December 2013.

6

HOW COMPANIES CAN REDUCE THEIR ENVIRONMENTAL FOOTPRINTS WHILE REMAINING PROFITABLE

Here we discuss how companies can reduce their environmental footprints while remaining profitable. Successful companies like Google, Lockheed Martin and 3M continually adapt to the future through innovations. Harnessing industrial adaptive capacity can also help conserve natural environmental resources, due to the opportunities for green manufacturing and services.

Nevertheless, there is still a place for proven messages about improving the efficiency of manufacturing. Early last century Henry Ford assembled existing technology, like the assembly line and interchangeable parts, to make the Model T car and sell it at a significantly lower price than his competition. By doing this he created a new and growing market. Also, by freezing the design of the Model T he was able to better refine the moving assembly line process, which in turn allowed him to cut costs further, lower prices even further, and drive the growth of the Ford Motor Company from manufacturing 10,000 cars in 1908 to 472,350 cars in 1915 to 933,720 cars in 1920 (21).

But, everything changed with the onset of the innovations introduced by General Motors (GM) in the 1920s. These took the direct opposite of Henry Ford's tack of "Any color … so long as it is black". The new approach is best summed up by the claim "A Car for Every Purse and Purpose", based on consumer research arranged by Alfred Sloan at GM. This company aimed to produce cars for distinct market segments aided by four activities; instalment payments, used car trade-ins, creation of closed car models and annual model changes. This required management of the diverse operations, which involved using financial statistics, such as return on investment, to ensure efficiency. He also established a pricing structure for models, which, from lowest to highest priced, were the Chevrolet, Pontiac, Oldsmobile, Buick and Cadillac. These models did not compete with each other, and buyers could be kept in the GM "family" as their buying power improved and preferences changed as they aged. These concepts, along with Ford's resistance to the change in the 1920s, propelled GM to have the highest sales of vehicles in the car industry by the early 1930s, a position it retained for over 70 years. Under Sloan's direction, GM became the largest industrial enterprise the world had ever known. Here innovation proved important, in the annual creation of new models (22).

GM is now planning a drastic shift over the next 10 years from global production platforms for 26 vehicles to just four by 2025, which could eventually save the company billions of dollars in production costs. The radical streamlining of GM's manufacturing architectures is intended to simplify the engineering and manufacturing of GM's future cars and trucks, while enabling the company to deliver better-differentiated designs more quickly to customers around the world. Again, innovation is important, along with improvements in efficiency (12).

In general, across all manufacturing sectors, there will be

four key areas for innovations; network-centric production, advanced materials, nano-manufacturing and mass customisation (4, 17). For network-centric production information technology will be integrated throughout manufacturing value chains. This will include developing 'smart' production processes that can be efficiently operated to optimise resources through production to recycling products at the end of their useful life. Smart control chips will be integrated into new process hardware during their development.

Advanced materials will be created using new supercomputer design systems, that are based on deep scientific knowledge about materials, like carbon. Design features for new materials will include desired strength, flexibility, weight and production cost. Technology will include synthetic biology, to explore biofabrication, such as biofabrication of human tissues and organs in the laboratory to replace diseased or damaged tissues of patients (13).

In nano-manufacturing nano-features will be embedded in products to raise their efficiency and performance. These products will range from high-efficiency solar cells and batteries, environmental control through filters based on nano-technology and medical applications based on nanobiosystems, to next-generation electronics and computing devices.

Mass customisation will involve producing small lots at a similar cost to current mass production. For example, small runs of products can be efficiently performed using three-dimensional printing, where complex products can be fabricated using powders, compared to traditional processes which use machine-tools and are expensive to setup.

To sustain innovative manufacturing in the future there is a clear need to reduce environmental footprints of manufacturing. This will involve technologies and systems that enable optimal utilisation of raw materials, energy, and resources, including areas as diverse as high performance catalysis, novel separations, and new reactor and waste management systems.

Traditionally waste management has concentrated on the last stage of the life cycle for commercial products, for manufacturing and packaging waste. This approach is currently peripheral to the mainstream economy and the only industry stakeholders are waste management companies.

In our new approach countries, including cities and regional areas, are to be resource sensitive. Countries will sustainably use resources. Companies will maximise efficiency and sustainability of manufacturing and service processes. They will:

- Minimise use of non-recyclable resources and minimise use of water and energy.
- Reuse recycle/treat resources.
- Remanufacture or recover parts.
- Close resource loops and make commodity loops: such as for metals.
- Make new products from recycled resources.
- Minimise disposal of resources to landfill and trade waste treatment.

This is an inclusive community and industry wide approach, unlike the past. Accompanying benefits can aid the competitiveness of industry. Also, we are beginning to more see wastes as resources, and in future be integrated into the mainstream economy.

How do we get to the future? Drivers for change are externalities and factors in business. An externality is defined as a benefit (or cost) which results from an activity or transaction by a company and which affects others outside the company. When companies sustainably make use of natural environments the benefits to all are conservation of natural resources, including maintaining the liveability of cities and towns.

In business drivers are to improve both efficiency and sustainability by reengineering manufacturing and service processes, with the aim for less waste, and to significantly reduces costs of this waste treatment/disposal. Businesses will also see new opportunities for innovative green products arising from the new approach to waste resources.

Minimising environmental footprints

Towards zero waste

To reduce waste we first need to identify all types of existing waste resource streams. This includes assessing hazards of waste to people and the environment and defining guidelines for each type of waste resource. Guidelines should aid minimising use of non-recyclable resources, reuse of waste resources, recycle and treatment of waste resources and minimising disposal of resources to landfill or trade waste treatment. Voluntary guidelines will initially arise from industry best practice, with governments slowly increasing costs of waste disposal to drive improved efficiency in the use of resources by industry.

Main types of waste are organic waste (such as green waste, food waste and oil waste), hazardous chemical waste (such as waste containing metals, solvents and other toxic chemicals) and hard waste (Plastic, glass, paper & cardboard, timber and wood products, leather and textiles, tyres and other rubber, electrical and electronic and masonry) and finally inseparable waste of mixed wastes.

Treatment options for organic waste include anaerobic digestion, composting, land fill and direct application to land. Anaerobic digestion of organic waste involves incubation of waste by microorganisms in tanks that are sealed to keep out air. These systems can aid energy recovery from capture of biogas produced by digestion and also reduce greenhouse emissions by gas capture. These systems can also improve microbial safety of organic products, which are valued as land fertilizers. Water companies may potentially assemble good business cases for co-digestion of organic wastes with domestic sewage at Waste Water Treatment Plants.

Composting of organic waste is a short-term solution due to emissions of greenhouse gases and high labour costs. Landfill is also a short-term solution, due to increasing costs for depositing waste at landfill sites. For applying untreated organic waste directly to land there are likely public health issues, which may limit this option.

Hazardous wastes include metals, solvents and other toxic chemicals. Recovery of hazardous waste components is the preferred option. Further options include destruction of toxic organic chemicals by microbes, most useful for decontaminating polluted soil and water and, finally, incineration of toxic chemicals or landfill. these last two are short term options due to rising costs of disposal.

Process reengineering

The Interface® carpet maker has reengineered its manufacturing processes to save water. In previous practice some carpet styles have taken up to 300 kg of water to dye one kg of carpet yarn. In the company's new process for making synthetic carpets nylon yarns are injected with colour at the point where they are extruded, rather than being dyed later. As a result, no water is used at this step and the carpets produced are more durable with less fade than water-dyed carpets. Also, old synthetic carpets can be completely recycled. Modular synthetic carpets can be made from 100% recycled yarn, sourced from the company's recycling program, which can include discarded fishing nets.

Remanufacturing and recovery of product parts

The Close the Loop Limited Company is a leading example for remanufacturing and recovery of parts. This company recycles inkjet cartridges, which would otherwise be disposed to landfill. The company first tests the electronic chips or reads serial numbers from cartridges to check reuse capabilities. Cartridges can be repacked for reuse or remanufacture or simply sent for destruction through another supplier. To repack cartridges, these are sorted by family groups or types, into approved shipping containers ready for return to nominated suppliers. The company works with Planet Ark (an Australian not-for-profit organisation with a vision of a world where people live in balance with nature) to provide a major network for recovering used cartridges and improve the community profile of the company.

As well as minimising waste manufacturing, processes will be designed to allow efficient extraction of chemical components from waste, such as metals. These, along with recycled components of products, will form economic loops as valuable ingredients for other manufacturers. So, these waste resources will form an important addition to the mainstream economy.

Making products so they can be recycled

It makes sense to design products that, at the end of their useful life, can be easily disassembled into individual types of materials and recycled. For example, the Celle Chair produced by the Herman Miller company is made of one-third recycled materials, and when its useful life is over, disassembles in a few minutes and is 99% recyclable.

New products from recycled materials

Recycling waste materials can lead to options for new products. The Close the Loop Limited Company has generated a novel wood substitute, called eWood®. This product is made from a mixture of plastics generated from waste recycling printer consumables. The eWood® product is suited for outdoor uses, being resistant to water, fungal rot, UV, insects and bacteria.

Leading change

A green manufacturer can influence suppliers to also reduce their environmental footprints. This can be formally done by using Environmental Product Declarations (EPDs). EPDs are statements from the company's suppliers that say how their materials are produced before the materials are bought. Suppliers must have a commitment to full disclosure of what is usually confidential information about how products are made. This is a standardised way of quantifying the environmental impact of a product or manufacturing system. Declarations include environmental impacts of a product through its life cycle of; raw material acquisition, energy use and efficiency, content of materials and chemical substances, emissions to air, soil and water and waste generation. Clinton Squires, managing director of Interface Australia, has reported that their EPDs met with resistance from some organisations, but most of the companies who now supply Interface tell them their environmental impacts have reduced, quality has improved and that they are now more profitable.

Green services

Service companies can also reduce their environmental footprints. Product distribution services can optimise transport runs, to minimise greenhouse gas emissions from transporting products. They can also optimise washing of vehicles to conserve water and reduce paper document requirements in delivery by using electronic signing. At head-office less paper documents can be used through electronic communication and storage. Buildings can be operated to minimise energy requirements, such as using intelligent lights in offices, that are only on when people are present.

Triple bottom line accounting

The triple bottom line (TBL) accounting system consists of three Ps: profit, people and planet. It aims to measure the financial, social and environmental performance of a corporation over a period of time. In this way the performance of a company is being measured based on its impact on society as a whole, both now and in the future. Only a company that produces a TBL is taking account of the full cost involved in doing business (20). Businesses, non-profit organisations and government departments alike can all use the TBL system.

The development of environmental accounting has been important to support TBL accounting. In environmental accounting traditional accounting methods and finance principles are utilised to compute the environmental costs of commercial and industrial decisions (11). For an individual company this allows assessing direct financial costs for the use of environmental resources or cost of remediating deleterious effects of manufacturing processes on natural environments and long term environmental consequences. Environmental accounting combined with modelling full life-cycles of products can be used to support decisions to reduce environmental footprints in ways that many company managers can easily understand. Externalities (Chapter 4) can also be quantified and addressed by environmental accounting. The use of environmental accounting can be a competitive advantage, as related to product quality (11).

It has been said that putting dollar prices on natural environmental resources indicates a rather narrow view of the values of natural environments. However, many business people readily understand the wider values of natural environments.

Case study: Orica, Australia

Over the last decade the chemical manufacturing company Orica, Australia, has planned to continually reduce its environmental footprint (15). Here we describe the results of this strategy, in change in energy consumption, greenhouse gas emissions, water consumption and waste production.

At Orica net energy consumption has risen on average by 8% per year since 2009, now at 22.7 M Gj, due to increased production. Nevertheless, the amount of energy used per tonne of products has been stable, at an average of about 4.5 GJ. The main energy source used by Orica is natural gas, 70% (both as fuel and feedstock), with 8% by electricity, 4% by diesel oil as a feedstock, and 18% by other sources.

While energy consumption at Orica has increased since 2009, greenhouse gas emissions have continually decreased over this time, with an average decrease of 7.5% per year (Figure 6.1). The total level of emissions in 2013 was 2.4 million tonnes of CO_2 equivalents. Orica's greenhouse gas profile is dominated by direct emissions of nitrous oxide, a by-product of nitric acid manufacture. The amount of greenhouse gas emissions per tonne of product has also decreased, by an average of 12.5% per year, with the level in 2013 of 0.5 tonnes of CO_2 equivalents per tonne of product.

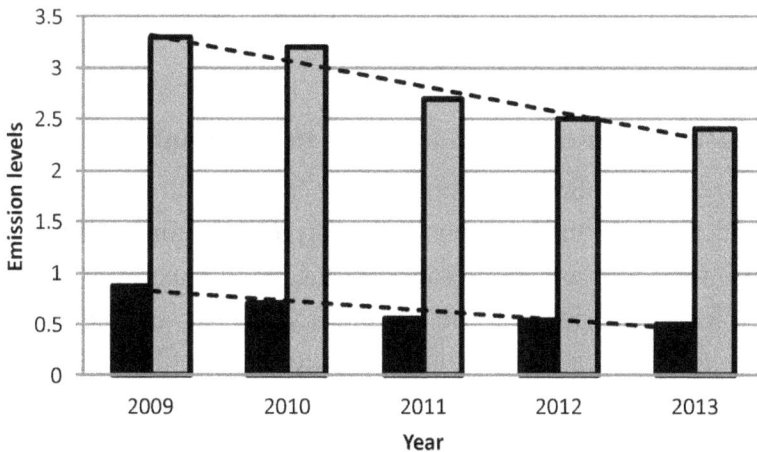

Figure 6.1 Decreases in greenhouse gas emissions at the chemical manufacturing company Orica, between 2009 and 2013. Black bars indicate total greenhouse gas emissions, million tonnes of CO2 equivalents per year; grey bars mark the amount of greenhouse gas emissions per tonne of product. Broken black lines are trend lines fitted to the data to illustrate decreases in these variables (15).

Following increased production, water consumption at Orica has also increased since 2009, with an average increase of 3.9% per year. Nevertheless, the amount of water used per tonne of product has decreased on average per year of 2.9% per tonne of product. The amount of water used per tonne of product in 2013 was 1.92 kL. The main source of water used by Orica is mains drinking water, 66%, with 19% for groundwater, 13% for surface water and 2% for recycled or waste water.

At Orica staff are also now working to minimise the amount of waste generated at its operations, prioritising activities to; eliminate or minimise waste streams where possible; increase opportunities for reuse and recycling; and treat and dispose waste where other options are not practicable. In 2013 Orica generated 16,900 tonnes of waste, of which 39% was classified as hazardous. This represents an increase of 2% from the 2012 result.

Release of industrial chemicals into the environment

A growing number of companies are working to reduce their chemical waste and to dispose of it correctly to minimise its effect on the environment. However, the rapid expansion of the chemical industries over the last thirty years has led to the production of increasing amounts of toxic waste effluents. There are around 60,000 chemicals in use around the world (2). This has led to an unprecedented exposure of the environment to a vast array of chemicals. While most of the chemicals in use are disposed of correctly, it is inevitable that significant quantities of many of these chemicals will be released into the environment, becoming pollutants. This may occur in a number of ways including (3):

- Accidental release of chemicals during their production and processing.
- Release of chemicals during their application.
- Accidental release of chemicals due to spillage.
- Deliberate release of the chemical into the environment, i.e. improper disposal.

Regulatory authorities, such as Environmental Protection Authorities in Australia and the USA, have been paying attention to reduce the contamination of the environment by industries. In the USA over 1,000 contaminated sites have been identified (Figure 6.2). Industrial companies are therefore becoming increasingly aware of the political, social, environmental and regulatory pressures to prevent escape of effluents into the environment. The occurrence of major incidents, such as the Union-Carbide (Dow) Bhopal disaster and the subsequent massive publicity due to the resulting environmental problems, has highlighted the potential for imminent and long-term disasters in the public's conscience (3). While policies and environmental efforts should continue to be directed towards applying pressure to industry to reduce toxic waste production, remediation technologies present opportunities to detoxify a whole range of industrial effluents, including those shown in Figure 6.2.

Once released into the environment, depending on the nature of the pollutant, the chemical can be found in air, soil and water. For example, benzene is typically found in the gaseous phase, while a metal contaminant (e.g. chromium) will be found largely in soils or sediments (3). Once released these pollutants may either be broken down or may persist in the environment until they are detected and quantified and their potential risk assessed.

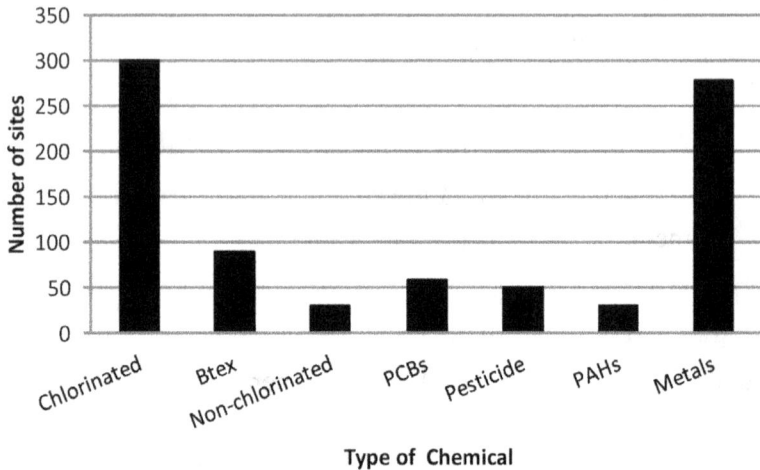

Figure 6.2 The number of contaminated sites in the USA, categorised by different types of toxic chemicals. Abbreviations: Btex, benzene, toluene, ethylbenzene, xylene; PCBs, polychlorinated biphenyl compounds; PAHs, poly aromatic hydrocarbons. These sites can be potentially detoxified by re-mediation technologies (3).

It may be that the pollutant(s) have to be removed and degraded, or degraded *in situ* (2).

Technologies available for removal of industrial contaminants from the environment

A number of options exist for the disposal (remediation) of pollutants found in the environment (3, 5). These include:

- **Incineration:** the process of the destruction of a pollutant through conversion to carbon dioxide and water via combustion.

- **Burying:** disposal of a pollutant by placing it in a sanitary landfill, which is engineered in a manner that protects the environment from the pollutant.

- **Solidification:** encapsulation of the pollutant in a solid matrix, like cement, which after hardening can be disposed of safely in a landfill.

- **Thermal desorption:** this technique utilises heat to increase the volatility of contaminants such that they can be removed from the soil.

- **Bioremediation:** The application of biological treatment to the clean-up of hazardous chemicals.

Next, we will focus on the sustainable remediation technology.

Bioremediation as an effective environmental friendly approach to removing industrial contaminants from the environment

The advantages of using bioremediation, rather than digging up the contaminated soil and placing in elsewhere, are that only moderate capital investment is required, as it only has low energy input. In addition, the processes are environmentally safe, do not generate waste, and are self-sustaining. In many cases bioremediation not only offers a permanent solution to the problem but also is cost effective. Cleaning up existing terrestrial environmental contamination in the United States alone may cost as much as one trillion dollars. Bioremediation can help reduce the costs of treatment as follows (2):

- *Treating contamination in place*: most of the cost associated with traditional clean-up technologies is associated with physically removing and disposing of contaminated soils. Because engineered bioremediation can be carried out in place by delivering nutrients to contaminated soils, it does not incur removal-disposal costs.

- *Harnessing natural processes*: at some sites, natural microbial processes can remove or contain contaminants without human intervention. In these cases, where intrinsic bioremediation (natural attenuation) is appropriate, substantial cost savings can be realised.

- *Reducing environmental stress*: because bioremediation methods minimise site disturbance compared with conventional clean-up technologies, post-clean-up costs can be substantially reduced.

As a technology bioremediation has a global application. In the UK alone it has been estimated that there are some 100,000 sites, which will cost between £10,000 million and £20,000 million to clean up. In terms of the bioremediation process, this depends greatly on the quality and quantity of the pollution and is affected by other factors such as the presence of toxic agents. Nevertheless, bioremediation is an applicable technology for a range of pollutants. Figure 6.3 shows the range of industries that use bioremediation as a technology (3).

Bioremediation Technologies available for removal of industrial contaminants from the environment

Three main types of methods are used in bioremediation of contaminated soils and water, which correspond to different ways of using micro-organisms to treat contaminates. These main types of methods are, monitored natural attenuation, *in situ* bioremediation and accelerated *in situ* bioremediation (3).

140

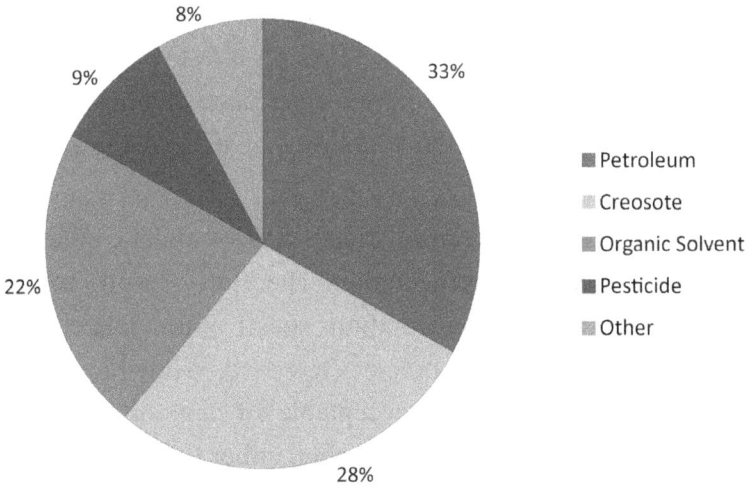

Figure 6.3 The range and weighting (as expressed as a percentage) of industries that utilise bioremediation (3).

Challenges to commercial use of bioremediation technologies

As we have seen, bioremediation offers the possibility of technically effective and relatively less expensive remediation. Assuming that the promise of bioremediation strategies are realised, why would anyone object to using these natural treatments? While bioremediation technology can be successfully applied to clean up contaminated sites, a failure to anticipate public issues can derail plans to deploy such technology (1). While some issues may revolve around technical aspects of bioremediation, others may derive from social concerns. Making decisions to apply bioremediation technology to a specific local site can usefully be viewed as a social process, that is informed by scientific and technical data, rather than as a physical process, that is only determined by scientific and technical data. While we do not claim that bioremediation represents a controversial technology, the use of an even simple clean-up option may become contro-versial (18). Bioremediation encompasses a suite of potential re-mediation options. Therefore, for a particular contaminated site, generic questions about the suitability of bioremediation may not be very useful.

To date there have been relatively few systematic studies of social responses to bioremediation. Therefore, despite increas-ing applications of bioremediation, social issues related to its deployment have not been properly assessed. While bioremedia-tion may prove to be socially acceptable for cleaning up contam-ination, it may not be fully acceptable, either across the suite of approaches it encompasses or across the range of sites at which it is proposed for deployment (7, 19). Acceptability evolves over time through interactions with individuals and organisations, and in response to successful cases of using bioremediation technol-ogy, along with related technical and non-technical information (9). To gain a better understanding of social acceptability issues and to improve our ability to predict outcomes in deliberations over the social acceptability of controversial technologies, it is useful to develop a conceptual framework for organising what was perceived to be the most important issues (23). A result-ing framework, PACT (Public Acceptability of Controversial Technologies) provides a common logic through which to view site-specific decision making about remediation technologies (Figure 6.4). This framework posits that making decisions about utilising remediation is a social process informed by scientific and technical information, rather than a science- or technology-driven process. PACT is built around dimensions that operate to influence decision-oriented dialogs over controversial remedia-tion technologies in any location.

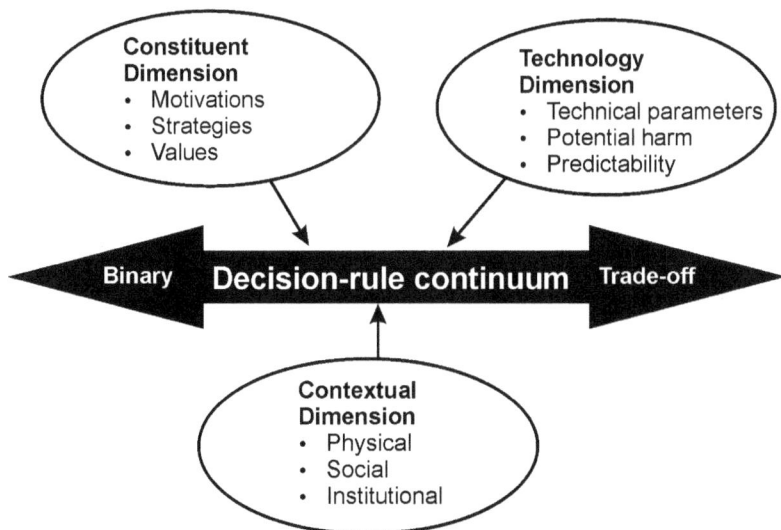

Figure 6.4 Overview of Public Acceptability of Controversial Technologies (PACT). This is used to assist in site-specific decision making about remediation technologies (23).

The factors relevant to specific decision settings and technologies varies from situation to situation. Although empirical data maybe scarce, applying PACT shows that a number of issues have the potential to impose conditions on the social acceptability of remediation, and that some issues could lead to acceptance or others to outright rejection. That is, PACT-based analysis focuses on an array of attributes that could strongly influence acceptability. In this context acceptability refers to participants' willingness to consider the technology in question as a viable alternative, rather than to whether the technology ultimately is to be deployed. Further, because many of these issues concern values and goals, they cannot be resolved simply by providing better or more detailed technical information about remediation. PACT is, therefore, instructive in showing how even seemingly benign or desirable technologies, such as remediation, have the potential to generate public controversies, and to delineate issues in ways that can help lead to their resolution.

Dr Kepa Morgan has also developed a general framework, the mauri model, for aiding decisions about proposed works that will affect natural environments, including remediation projects (14, 16). The mauri model is able to show the holistic effects of a project under four key criterial dimensions; community, culture, environment and economic:

- **Community:** wellbeing of community, including public health and safety, social wellbeing, and economic wellbeing.
- **Culture:** integrity of culture in terms of the identity and prestige of local indigenous groups.
- **Environment:** integrity of the ecosystem and natural resources.
- **Economic:** costs and functional and technical applicability of proposed options.

The mauri model provides a culturally-based framework, within which indigenous values are explicitly profiled alongside Western knowledge. This includes identifying the cultural relationship of local indigenous groups with local land and seascapes.

There are two main applications of this approach: to assess worldviews of each stakeholder group in relation to the issue at hand, and to determine the effect of each proposed project option on the four criterial dimensions.

For each major stakeholder a worldview analysis can be undertaken, to help understand what each group considers to be the important factors in deciding the best project option. Stakeholders may include government agencies, local companies, and local communities, including indigenous peoples. The analysis provides a general understanding of what each major stakeholder group considers important when choosing an option, by assessing their views on the value for each criterial dimension. The analysis shows the relative degree of priority each stakeholder group gives for each criterial dimension. This allows identifying where there are major differences in views, and so where discussion can best be focussed to promote a consensus. In part, stakeholder groups are assisted to better understand the limitations of their own worldviews, essential in terms of fairly recognising the values of others.

The mauri model is then used to explore the effects of the proposed options on the four criterial dimensions, by identifying indicators for each criterion, and how these will be influenced by the options. It is also optimal that the indicators be agreed by the stakeholders, in terms of promoting consensus on the results of analysis. Changes in the indicators are determined semi-quantitatively, according to the five-points 'mauri-o-meter' scale. Changes can be assessed for the present, the past, and forecast for the future. That is, some impacts have long-term effects. In addition, in the absence of specific environmental data alternative information can be used to estimate past effects, for instance, in resource management and planning documentation, indigenous knowledge of the area, and known contemporary preferences evident in terms of priority of locations for recreation and commercial tourism activities.

To determine the absolute sustainability of an option, the indicator scores are then averaged, with equal weight given to each dimension. The mauri model, therefore, can be used to compare the proposed options and the status quo (no action). That is, a cost-benefit analysis. A key advantage of this framework, then, is to easily assess financial project costs against intangible benefits for community, culture and environmental criteria. It can also give an understanding of how the proposed options can be improved, or if additional options are needed.

Among a range of applications, the mauri model has been applied to aid decisions on options to remediate the wreck of the MV Rena ship, which ran aground on the Otaiti reef, near Tauranga, New Zealand, in 2011. This event resulted in major oil contamination of the local environment (6, 10).

Conclusion

Countries, including cities and regional areas, are to be resource sensitive. Countries will sparingly use non-renewable resources, and recycle others. Innovative manufacturing in the future will include reduction of environmental footprints of manufacturing. Companies will maximise efficiency and sustainability of manufacturing and service processes, while remaining profitable. Innovative manufacturing will involve process reengineering, remanufacturing and recovery of product parts, make products that can be easily recycled, and make new products from recycled resources. Wastes will be seen as resources, and be integrated into the mainstream economy. For example, the international chemical manufacturer Orica has significantly decreased both its greenhouse gas emissions and water use per tonne of product over the last five years.

Manufacturing and service companies will use Triple Bottom Line accounting systems, including environmental accounting to support decisions to reduce environmental footprints. For manufacturing companies this will be combined with modelling full life-cycles of products.

Due to past and continuing industrial manufacturing processes there exists large areas of the world where contaminated land can be found, which constitute major environmental and health hazards. Bioremediation offers the opportunity to utilise natural microbial populations to treat a contaminated site, which returns the elements making up the contaminants to natural nutrient cycles. This technology provides a number of options for treating different types of contaminants and different sites. Nevertheless, one of the main limitations to the use of this technology is social acceptance. In each particular case the local community should be consulted about its potential concerns and these views used to inform the decision to apply bioremediation to clean up a contaminated site.

In the following chapter we discuss how manufacturing and service companies can be helped to reduce their environmental footprint though the setting up of independent local task forces.

References

1. Axelrod, L. (1994) Balancing personal needs with environmental preservation: Identifying the values that guide decisions in ecological dilemmas. *Journal of Social Issues*, 50(3): 85-104.
2. Ball, A.S. and K.K. Kadali (2012) The removal of toxic waste. *Microbiology*, 2112(9): 97-99.
3. Ball A.S. (2007). Terrestrial Environments, Soils and Bioremediation. In: *The SAGE Handbook of Environment and Society*. Sage Publications, London, pp. 385-394.

4. Bonvillian, W.B. (2013) Advanced manufacturing policies and paradigms for innovation. *Science*, 342: 1173-1175.

5. Cookson, J.T. (1995) *Bioremediation Engineering; Design and Application*. McGraw Hill, New York.

6. Commissioners (2016) Decision of Panel on MV Rena Resource Consent Applications. Volume One. Date of Decision: 26 February 2016. Bay of Plenty Regional Council, New Zealand.

7. Davison, A., I. Barns, and R. Schibeci (1997) Problematic publics: a critical review of surveys of public attitudes to biotechnology. *Science Technology and Human Values*, 22(3): 317-348.

8. Dunk, A.S. (2007). Assessing the Effects of Product Quality and Environmental Management Accounting on the Competitive Advantage of Firms. *Australasian Accounting Business and Finance Journal*, 1(1): 28-38.

9. Eagly, A., and P. Kulsea (1997) Attitudes, attitude structure and resistance to change. In: *Environment, Ethics, and Behavior: The Psychology of Environmental Valuation and Degradation*. pp. 122-153.

10. Fa'aui, T.N. and T.K. Morgan (2014) Restoring the Mauri to the Pre- Mv Rena state. *MAI Journal*, 3(1): 3-17.

11. Frost, G.R. and T.D. Wilmhurst (1998) Evidence of environmental accounting in Australian companies. *Asian Review of Accounting*, 6(2): 163-180.

12. Klayman, B. and P. Lienert (2-10-2014) Analysis – GM's 2025 platform plan: Simplify and seek to save billions. *Reuters*. http://uk.reuters.com, accessed 7-10-14.

13. Mironov, V., T. Trusk, V. Kasyanov, S. Little, R. Swaja and R. Markwald (2009). Biofabrication: a 21st century manufacturing paradigm. *Biofabrication*, 1, 022001.

14. Morgan, T.K. (2004) A Tangata Whenua Perspective on Sustainability using the Mauri Model. Towards decision making balance with regard to our social, economic, environmental and cultural well-being.

15. Orica (2013) Sustainability Report. http://www.orica.com, accessed 7-10-14.

16. Ormsby, T. and T.K. Morgan (2015) Whangapoua Harbour Mauri Model Analysis. http://www.maramatanga.co.nz/project/whangapoua-harbour-mauri-model-analysis, accessed 3-3-17.

17. President's Council of Advisors on Science and Technology (2012) Report to the President on capturing domestic competitive advantage in advanced manufacturing. Executive Office of the President. http://www.whitehouse.gov, accessed 30-1-14.

18. Priest, S.H. (1994) Structuring public debate on biotechnology: Media frames and public response. *Science Communication*, 16(2): 166-179.

19. Stern, P.C. and T. Dietz (1994) The value basis of environmental concern. *Journal of Social Issues*, 50 (3): 65-84.

20. *The Economist* (2009) Triple bottom line. It consists of three Ps: profit, people and planet http://www.economist.com, accessed 17-8-16.

21. Vlaskovits, P. (2011) Henry Ford, Innovation, and That "Faster Horse" Quote. HBR Blog Network. http://blogs.hbr.org, accessed 7-10-14.

22. Wikipedia (24-8-2014) Alfred P. Sloan. http://en.wikipedia.org/wiki/Alfred_P._Sloan, accessed 7-10-14.

23. Wolfe, A.K. and D.J. Bjornstad (2002) Why Would Anyone Object? An Exploration of Social Aspects of Phytoremediation Acceptability. *Critical Reviews in Plant Sciences*, 21(5):429-438.

7

CONCLUSION AND ACTIONS:
How agriculture and industry can become stakeholders for conservation of natural environments

Here we discuss how agriculture and industry can become stakeholders for conservation of natural environments and how to build mutual respect between environmental groups and agriculture and industry.

Farmers and agricultural, manufacturing and service companies provide essential supporting activities for human life on Earth. Continuation of life on Earth, however, demands that these groups minimise their environmental footprints. In practical terms, these groups must reduce their environmental impacts and at the same time contain, or even reduce, costs. It has been argued here that farms and manufacturing and service companies are mostly involved in activities that are linked to natural environmental resources, like air, water, soil and energy sources. So, to ensure there is a future for further generations, with a high quality of life, dedicated strategies of cooperation must be adopted now.

What actions can agricultural companies and farmers take?
Over the last few decades agricultural managers have moved strongly toward evidence-based methods, building on scientific

knowledge and capability for analysis to define adaptive changes in the face of variable climatic factors. In particular, there has been a better understanding of soil, water and various ecological cycles, especially those involving carbon compounds. Thus, farmers are well placed to continue to make adaptations, for instance, in the event of climate change.

To monitor – and soon reduce – the environmental footprint of the farm unit, we stress the value of shared experience, of farmers being in touch with other groups. The existence of supportive organisations, has been an essential element in the past: sometimes simply gatherings of the farmers themselves, like local farmers associations, and at other times external organisations. It is essential that such networks continue and are strengthened: sometimes with national Farmers Federations, sometimes with government departments and agencies, and sometimes with R & D bodies, such as local universities. From time to time there will be substantial time-bounded task-defined development across agency task forces with specific remits, such as across large water catchment areas. The overall modus operandi will be to think globally and act locally. These activities must result in constantly updating best practice to minimise environmental impacts.

The historic collaboration with developing countries must continue, albeit with at times more emphasis on the efforts of the local people to improve agricultural yields and related practical matters. For developing countries the long-standing links with United Nations Food and Agriculture Organisation, the Centre for International Agricultural Research, and the Crawford Fund, must be maintained.

Agricultural managers need to develop and communicate innovative 'know' knowledge and practice to reduce environmental footprints of farms, while addressing climate change, and the global need to improve agricultural food yields. In doing this it is also of vital importance that agricultural companies and farmers are recognised publicly for their work to reduce their negative impacts on natural environments and their help to conserve these resources. Here agriculture will be seen as a key part of the environment, as well as the economy.

What action can manufacturing and service companies take?

For immediate impact on their environmental footprints, many companies can still save energy, with the twin 'goods' of reducing operational costs and reducing climate change, while remaining profitable. By saving energy companies can directly act to reduce their impact on climate change, and also reduce operational costs. In the USA the main human activities producing greenhouse gas are electricity generation (38%), transportation (31%), manufacturing industry (14%) residential (6%) and service companies (4%) (15). Similar data has been reported for other developed countries. Clearly both manufacturing and service companies currently make significant contributions to greenhouse gas emissions.

Companies can meet the challenge to reduce their contributions to greenhouse gas emissions and otherwise minimise their environmental footprints, while maintaining profitability. To do this companies can harness their industrial adaptive capacity. Successful companies generally continually adapt to future challenges through innovation.

Also, accounting staff can report on the direct value of environmental resources to the company, using environmental accounting methods to identify resource use, monitor and measure costs of a company's impact on the environment, as a key part of Triple Bottom Line accounting (Chapter 6).

Improved green manufacturing processes and services will be the key sectors for creation of economic wealth in the future (Chapter 6). Manufacturers can reengineer manufacturing processes to reduce resource needs and environmental impacts. R&D support can often be obtained from government sources. Product distribution services can optimise transport runs, optimise washing of vehicles (frequency and process), reduce paper document requirements (electronic signing), and improve efficiency of cold storage. Head offices can reduce paper document requirements (electronic communication and storage) and reduce energy requirements.

Companies can gain generic support through industry associations. In the past there has been collaboration between industry associations and Environment Protection Authorities to reduce environmental footprints through technical innovations and improved operational processes, for instance in Australia. In general, to help manufacturing and service companies further reduce their environmental footprints, while reducing costs and gaining better innovation products and services, we recommend these companies work through their local industry associations.

We also propose that these companies can gain wider support and knowledge from alternative sources that are collected in an independent task force, at city, regional or state levels in each country. The group might have a name like, 'Task Force for Sustainable Manufacturing and Services'. The role of the task force would be to agree a forward strategy and its implementation. As well as including industry associations members of the task force should also include all other key stakeholder groups: namely, relevant local government departments (business and environment), local Environmental Protection Authority or its local office, and local Universities (with research and knowledge capabilities in manufacturing, and natural environments, including environmental accounting). Here manufacturing and service companies will be seen as key parts of the environment, as well as the economy.

It is important to recognise companies in each industry association that are already pro-actively reducing their environmental footprints. These companies are most likely to lead change within their own association. In some areas the local Environmental Protection Authority may have had previous experience in working with industry associations to reduce waste issues, a process which could be used to fulfil the objectives of this book.

A key role for the industry associations is to bench mark best current practice for minimising waste and greenhouse gas emissions. Industry associations can also identify research needs to help re-engineer manufacturing processes to reduce environmental impacts. The research needs may be company specific, to be dealt with in-house, or of generic interest for the association, which may include collaboration with university researchers.

The task force should set up a website to promote action and increase public knowledge about how industries are reducing their environmental footprints. Another potential task is reviewing regulations and working with government to update regulations in line with the new approach. One approach is to set regulatory limits on disposal of waste at a minimum level. So, well performing companies will have waste well below the regulatory limits, while poor performers may produce waste contaminants above regulatory limits and so have to pay fees and or fines. By facing financial penalties poor performing companies can be persuaded to improve their environmental performance. Over time as companies gradually reduce their waste amounts of contaminants, while limits on disposal of contaminants can be gradually decreased. In this way, good companies will always be ahead of regulatory requirements.

In a similar way, the cost for disposing waste at local landfill sites can be gradually increased to help drive change of poor performing companies. For example, the general levy for disposal of industrial and municipal waste to landfill in metropolitan and provincial areas in the State of Victoria, Australia, has recently increased by 10% per year (2011-2015), with subsequent lower but significant increases planned (4), see Figure 7.1. In Victoria additional costs are required for disposal of prescribed wastes, that contain significant levels of heavy metals and or toxic organic chemicals. Also, a company that produce wastes with very high levels of contaminants must treat the waste on site, and not be allowed to dispose this waste to landfill.

First steps for the task force should be to help companies reduce water and energy requirements, to reduce manufacturing and service costs. This would give companies a direct benefit for being part of the new approach. For manufacturing a major area of focus will be energy efficient manufacturing processes — where manufacturing processes that consume high levels of energy can be substituted by alternatives that use energy more efficiently, and therefore reduce operational costs.

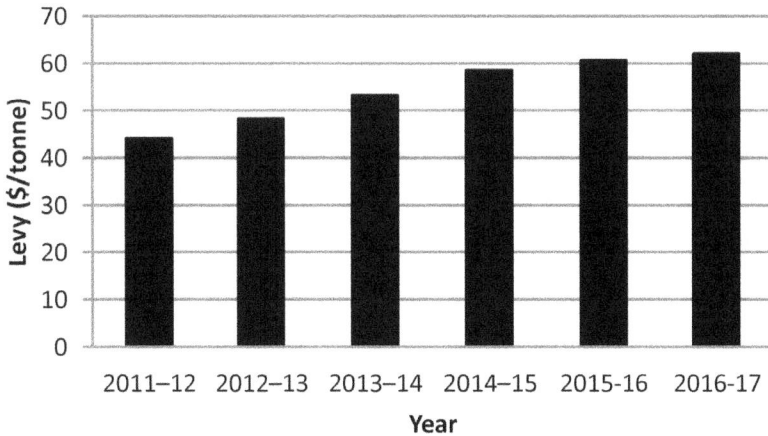

Figure 7.1: Increases in landfill levies for disposal of industrial and municipal waste to landfill in metropolitan and provincial areas, Victoria, Australia (4).

Agriculture and Industry as key stakeholders to support conservation of natural environmental resources and climate

With agricultural and industrial companies taking responsibility for their parts of the global environment it will be natural for them to more publicly support conservation of natural environments. The more difficult task, but one that must be addressed throughout, is to convince environmental interest lobby groups that this industry collaboration has practical outcomes and is not simply a defence mechanism. This communication issue is further discussed later.

Companies can indirectly reduce emissions of greenhouse gases by supporting strategies to reduce emissions from electricity generation. We need to move from fossil energy resources to renewable energy, but how do we do this? Together electricity generation and transportation emit the majority of total emissions of greenhouse gases in developed countries, and therefore are essential areas for attention.

To electricity production systems with low greenhouse gas emissions

We are looking for electricity production systems that abundantly supply electricity with low-emissions, and that are economically achievable. There are several contenders, some proven to be economically, and some not. Emissions from a range of different energy producers are shown in Figure 7.2. Of the lowest emitters nuclear power is the only type that is known to provide continual base electricity supply. However, nuclear power systems are expensive to set up, and in some countries, like Australia, lack public support.

Coal is currently the cheapest energy source in many countries, but has the highest emissions of all major energy sources. It has been proposed that coal can be combined with capture of emitted carbon dioxide and storage, but this is unproven on a commercial scale, so we cannot rely on it yet.

To provide continual power from renewable systems with lowest emissions, wind and solar, these could be combined with energy banks, most likely geothermal systems. Nevertheless, research and development of these combined systems is needed to show proven stability of electricity supply at large scale. In the meantime natural gas could be an intermediate fuel. Natural gas gives substantially lower emissions than black coal (470 compared to 1000 g CO_2/kWH_e) and has proven economic utilisation and operational technology. So, as argued by Alan Finkel, natural gas provides a practical intermediate source of energy

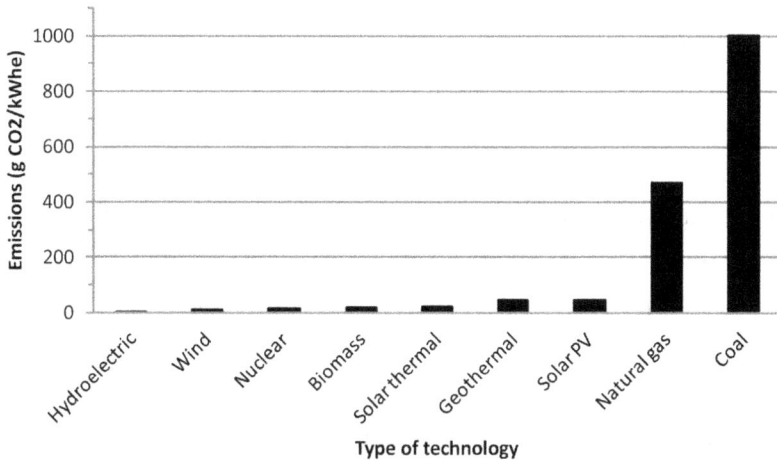

Figure 7.2 Greenhouse gas emissions for different electricity sources. Explanation of sources: Hydroelectric power is electricity derived from the energy of falling water or fast running water; Wind power is the use of air flow through wind turbines to mechanically power generators for producing electricity; Nuclear power is the use of nuclear reactions that release nuclear energy to generate heat, which most frequently is then used in steam turbines to produce electricity; Biomass means the use of biological cells, such as yeast or algae, grown on cheap food sources; low emission biomass system technologies include pyrolysis (burning of biomass in the absence of oxygen), and anaerobic digestion (where microbes produce methane -biogas- by breaking down biomass material, also in the absence of oxygen, then burning the biogas), followed by conversion of heat to electricity; Solar thermal means direct heating of water by sunlight collectors, with heat converted to electricity; Geothermal power is electricity generated from thermal energy generated and stored in the Earth; Solar PV means conversion of sunlight to electrical energy using photovoltaic panels; Power from natural gas or coal is produced by burning the material to produce heat which is then converted to electricity (data source: 11).

in the course of reducing greenhouse gas emissions (5). Natural gas then could be used as an intermediate fuel to generate base electricity while renewable energy systems are proven to provide base electricity supplies.

To provide transport systems with low greenhouse gas emissions

An electricity supply system with low emissions will optimally support electrical power systems for cars, buses and trucks. Electrical cars and buses, which connect to main electricity supplies to top up batteries, have been available for some time. Currently these have limited travel distances of electric vehicles before needing top ups, though companies are working to improve the capabilities of these.

Currently there are no commercial renewable energy systems for aeroplanes, large ships and tankers, due to the needs for high energy sources. Nevertheless hydrogen, a non-emitting fuel, can be used to power aircraft (2). In 2008, a light aircraft powered by a hydrogen fuel cell achieved straight-level flight on a manned mission. A large commercial hydrogen powered aircraft could be built by 2020-2040. To reduce emission of greenhouse gases the hydrogen fuel should be produced using low-emission main energy systems, as discussed above.

Better energy efficiency with clean cooking stoves

The Global Alliance for Clean Cookstoves aims to provide 100 million households with clean-burning cooking stoves by 2020 in developing countries. The purpose of this campaign is to achieve improvements in the quality and stability of the global environment, as well as for human health, livelihoods and gender empowerment (3, 6, 12, 13). Performance data indicates that the rocket-type of cooking stoves is a substantial improvement on traditional types of low-technology stoves, in terms of thermal efficiency, and reduced emissions of toxic black carbon particles and carbon monoxide. Black carbon, though short lived, is also the strongest absorber of solar radiation in the atmosphere and so contributes significantly to global warming. Also, while gas and liquid fuels represent the cleanest current household energy sources, these and other clean fuels are currently either not available or prohibitively expensive in many areas in developing countries. Nevertheless, use of cheap biomass fuels, such as animal dung and wood, can approach the performance of gas and liquid fuels. This is a major advantage as about 3 billion poor people in developing countries, who subsist on a daily income of less than $2 a day, rely on solid biomass fuels for cooking and space heating, using traditional stoves, contribute to about 50% of the anthropogenic emissions of black carbon.

The Global Alliance for Clean Cookstoves also supports a new innovative approach to reducing greenhouse gas emissions and improving human health, by Project Surya. Here selected people using stoves in poor regions of India have been given mobile phones, with satellite connections, to provide field data on fuel consumption and pollutant emissions in real-time. This data is used to estimate the climate gains from reduced emissions from cook stoves for short-lived climate pollutants such as black carbon, ozone and methane. as well as carbon dioxide. Project Surya will then distribute the funds from climate credits directly to the participants through local rural banks, which can be used by people to offset the cost of buying a more efficient stove.

Investing in the future

Like any other sector, the clean energy sector depends increasingly on funding from the capital investment markets. The more we invest in it the quicker the technology like solar, wind and geothermal power will effectively reduce the risk of climate change.

Holders of investments, such as pension and superannuation funds and university endowment funds, must take responsibility for both the future returns and impacts of their investments. Investment funds hire asset managers to look after their investments. One of the difficulties increasingly being encountered by many asset managers is the difference between their longer-term fiduciary responsibilities and the much shorter-term focus on returns. Currently these asset managers are mostly rewarded on short-term gains. However, investment funds and other asset owners are commonly running a significant risk by ignoring the likely future effect of climate change and limits of non-renewable energy sources on the financial performances of traditional energy companies. Globally investment funds currently put 55 per cent of their funds in carbon-exposed industries, and less than 2 per cent of their funds in low-carbon energy and other industries (7).

Nevertheless, a growing number of investment owners, about 170 by 2014, have divested funds from major coal, oil and gas producers and put more of their funds into renewable energy companies. These forward-thinking investment owners include the Darwin Superannuation Fund, the city of Oakland in California, the British Medical Association, the Quakers, and educational institutions like Stanford University and the Australian National University. Supporting this change in focus for investments is the Divest-Invest movement, founded three years ago. Its goal is to encourage institutions, foundations, charities, wealthy individuals – in fact anyone with investments – to commit to taking them out of industries that promote use of fossil fuels and to putting into the clean energy sector (1).

Roles for government

The move to green technology can be seen as promoting wide-ranging effects on society, like the revolution in information and communication technology. Therefore, there is a place for governments to stimulate investments in green technology. Here we will see public and private investments working together in synergistic fashion, for example, to enable transformation of existing energy infrastructure. Governments also have a role to manage the changes in skills required, through education policy. This includes addressing imbalances in labour markets following the changes in technology (10). For example, both vocational education and higher education have been highly supported by Australian federal governments over the last two decades, in response to skill and knowledge requirements (8, 9, 14).

Breaking the impasse

To break the current impasse, in part we require mutual respect of environmental activists on one hand, and mainstream agriculture/industry and government on the other. This could be promoted by meetings between leaders of environmental groups, and leaders of agriculture and industry, with a view to agree on collective action to conserve the global environment. Universities may provide a neutral place for meetings with the different groups. By working together we are most likely to gain more rapid responses to environmental issues.

How can community supporters of natural environments be involved?

General community members should recognise when a local farm or company is helping to save energy, water or other environmental resources in a positive way. However, at many points in the operation of farms and factories and other commercial systems there is public misunderstanding of the processes and expectation that things like so-called waste or misuse of chemicals could be avoided. Also, for far too long, good work by many companies to reduce their impacts on natural environments has often gone under the radar, or has been seen as just by self-interest.

As discussed in chapter 5, many agricultural practices have both upsides and downsides. Ongoing research is needed to identify and reduce negative effects. Farmers' use of cultivation to kill weeds is a good example of new knowledge and technology and adaptive behaviour, to improve efficiency while reduce negative impacts.

Years ago when land was being cultivated to prepare for sowing a crop each substantial fall of rain at pre-sowing times led to germination of weeds. Then at each time a cultivation was needed to kill as many of these weeds as possible. During cultivation the tractor burnt fuel and inadvertently generated a lot of carbon dioxide. Also, through aerating the soil some soil nitrogen was made available, which caused oxygenation of the carbon in the soil organic matter, and so released even more carbon dioxide. In later times farmers used a chemical spray to kill the weeds, applied at a precise rate by an operated unit from a lightweight tractor. This change produced much less carbon dioxide and also improved soil structure. But, as an excellent illustration of the need for actively reviewing changes, it was later realised that field management in the years leading up to cropping could greatly reduce seed setting of weeds. Subsequently, farmers realised that if the mulch left by the first crop was left on the ground after cropping there was much less germination of weed seeds. Later on, agricultural suppliers developed a spray unit for tractors which was activated by recognition of weeds through an onboard camera. With this new process farmers could apply much less chemical weedicide than previously. Though this series of improvements in agricultural practice seems quite complex, it is important to have such efforts understood, as a knowledge-based improvement in both farming efficiency and reduction of environmental impacts.

In industry we have seen similar examples of knowledge-based increases in manufacturing efficiency while reducing environmental impacts, as illustrated in Chapter 6.

Getting the message out

A key to optimally utilise the new approach will be communication and networking, both at the local and global levels. People will use websites and other internet resources, like Facebook and Twitter, to broadcast new stories about collaborations of industry and agriculture with the community, to help conserve environments on our planet. Schools, community centres and town halls will invite local farmers and industry leaders to tell people how they are reducing their environmental footprints, and to promote discussion and give feedback. Here is a place for local government to be involved.

Conclusion

A step-wise approach to reducing the environmental footprints of industry and agriculture is the best way to get all stakeholders on board. For example, to start with reducing energy and water requirements, and in changing energy sources for electricity generation natural gas should be the first choice to replace coal, while renewable energy sources are developed to provide base electricity loads in the future.

Previously created strategies can be included in the new approach, such as the electric planet and development of appropriate technologies for developing countries, like Clean Cookstoves. Appropriate technologies should be manufactured locally to improve employment and give local communities a stake in helping to respond to environmental issues like climate change.

A key action is to develop mutual respect between environmental group leaders and agriculture and industry leaders. Also, as agricultural and industrial companies become stakeholders for conserving natural environments we will gain better responses to environmental issues, including climate change.

This new inclusive way to improving responses to environmental issues, and therefore sustainable life on planet earth for future generations, can apply to both developing and developed countries. To save plant Earth there is a role for everyone interested in supporting industry and agriculture to reduce their environmental footprints.

References

1. Arbib, J. (2014) Organisations controlling £30bn are divesting from fossil fuels. *The Guardian*, U.K., 23-9-14. http://www.the-guardian.com, accessed 20-10-14.

2. BBC (4-4-2008) Hydrogen-powered plane takes off. http://news.bbc.co.uk, accessed 9-1-17.

3. Berkeley Air Monitoring Group. (2012) Stove Performance Inventory Report. Prepared for the Global Alliance for Clean Cookstoves, United Nations Foundation. http://berkeleyair.com/publications/, accessed 9-1-17.

4. Environmental Protection Authority Victoria (2013) Landfill and prescribed waste levies. http://www.epa.vic.gov.au, accessed 6-1-17.

5. Finkel, A. (2013) The Electric Planet. http://electricplanet.com/, accessed 7-10-14.

6. Global Alliance for Clean Cookstoves. http://cleancookstoves.org/, accessed 9-1-17.

7. Hewson, J. (2014). Reaction to ANU's move is excessive. *Financial Review*, 17-10-2014. http://www.afr.com, accessed 20-10-14.

8. Howard, J. (2004) Election Speech 2004, Brisbane, Queensland, Australia, 26 September 2004. http://electionspeeches.moadoph.gov.au, accessed 28-10-14.

9. Keating, P. (1996) Speech by The Prime Minister, The Hon P J Keating, MP, Australian Education Union Annual Federal Conference, Melbourne, Victoria, Australia, 19 January 1996. http://pmtranscripts.dpmc.gov.au, accessed 28-10-14.

10. Mazzucato, M. (2013). *The entrepreneurial state. Debunking public vs. private sector myths*. Anthem Press.

11. Moomaw, W., P. Burgherr, G. Heath, M. Lenzen, J. Nyboer and A. Verbruggen, (2011) Annex II: Methodology. In IPCC. *Special Report on Renewable Energy Sources and Climate Change*

Mitigation, eds. O. Edenhofer, R. Pichs-Madruga, Y. Sokona, K. Seyboth, P. Matschoss, S. Kadner, T. Zwickel, P. Eickemeier, G. Hansen, S. Schlömer and C. von Stechow. Cambridge University Press, Cambridge, United Kingdom and New York, NY, USA. http://www.ipcc.ch/report/srren/, accessed 9-1-17.

12. Project Surya. http://www.projectsurya.org/, accessed 7-10-14.

13. Project Surya (2012) Pilot Carbon Credit Market. http://www.projectsurya.org/ , accessed 7-10-14.

14. Rudd, K. (2007) Rudd Calls For An "Education Revolution", Melbourne Education Research Institute at the University of Melbourne, Melbourne, Victoria, Australia, 23 January 2007, http://australianpolitics.com/, accessed 28-10-14.

15. U.S. Environmental Protection Agency (2013) Inventory of U.S. Greenhouse Gas Emissions and Sinks: 1990-2011. United Nations Framework on Climate Change. National Inventory Submissions 2013. EPA 430-R-13-001. http://unfccc.int/national_reports/, accessed 9-1-17.

AUTHOR BIOGRAPHIES

Dr Duncan Rouch is a strategic and policy planner and independent scientist. His main expertise is in the education and environmental sectors. He has over 25 years of experience as a professional research scientist. As well has having worked at universities in both the UK and Australia he also has experience in government and industry. He has over 70 research publications, in scientific journals and books.

The late **Dr David Smith AM** was a senior Australian agricultural scientist who has filled just about every role in agriculture in the local, national and international spheres. He crawled out into the ecosystems of the home farm, learning about them from a young age. He was trained in plant ecology as well as agronomy, taking a Masters degree in Australian native vegetation ecology and a Ph. D. in the ecology of the southern Australian pasture complex. Thus, he has worked at the inter-action of human managed agriculture and the natural environment. He has been Director-general of Agriculture in Victoria, and chair of many public bodies and R&D groups, including cotton, when GM cotton was produced.

For his service to agriculture he was made a Member of the Order of Australia in 2013.

Professor Andrew Ball has over 25 year's research experience in environmental microbiology. He started his career as a Research Fellow in Liverpool University and more recently held the position of Reader at the University of Essex, UK where he was a member of staff for 16 years. In 2005 he was appointed Foundation Chair of Environmental Biotechnology at Flinders University and Director of Flinders Bioremediation. Professor Ball brings a wealth of research and teaching experience to Victoria in the fields of algal biotechnology, bioremediation, organic waste treatment and environmental microbiology. In January 2012, Andrew was appointed Professor of Environmental Biotechnology at RMIT University and from November 2013 as Director of the newly formed Centre for Environmental Sustainability and Remediation (EnSuRe).